MW00647728

"TIME TO MAKE gives us the pep talk we need to just get started. If I wasn't laughing out loud, I was singing 'amen sister!' I would recommend this book to anyone who has ever struggled with getting started making something and who needs a reminder of what 'making' really means."

Emily Waechtler, Designer
BLUE CORDUROY

"Although I've been making for most of my life, Ginger's book helped me uncover why, at times, I drag my creative feet. Her words have a way of building confidence and imparting a real 'can-do' attitude for any and all future making projects. I'm feeling certain the 'failure fairy' has been banned from my head."

Marj. Kocher, Artist
GOBLETS BY MARJ

"Ginger's book feels like the moment your friend says something to you that surprises your despair-tears into becoming suddenly-attentive, ready-to-laugh shiny eyes."

Molly Ledford, Singer/Songwriter
LUNCH MONEY

TIME to MAKE

TIME to MAKE

throw yourself at your
creative life

don't wait

GINGER HENDRIX

american
rookie books

Copyright © 2014 by Ginger Hendrix.

All rights reserved. No part of this publication may be reproduced, distributed or transmitted in any form or by any means, including photocopying, recording, or other electronic or mechanical methods, without the prior written permission of the publisher, except in the case of brief quotations embodied in critical reviews and certain other noncommercial uses permitted by copyright law.

Time to Make/ Ginger Hendrix. — 1st ed.
ISBN 9780692024614

Cover design by deLlamas Design & Graphics
Cover photo by A Blake Photography

For Dorothy Cuffel
(1914 – 2002)

—the best, bold claimer I ever knew.

TABLE OF CONTENTS

NO FAIRY DUST

INDEXES & LISTS

PROLOGUE:
THIS MIGHT BE THE REAL REASON
WE DON'T MAKE TIME

I 'm about to tell you how I'm always talking with people at wedding cheese tables about risk taking. How I tell them it's so important. How we need to worry about our perfectionism less and embrace our making lives more.

Also, I'm going to tell you that people tell me I'm brave. (Well, I mean, people who don't know me very well.)

But please know that I've found bravery to be tricky business. It doesn't always feel the way you think it would.

There's a sort of lesser-known part of trying out bravery: because even when we claim it, it doesn't always make us feel particularly heroic.

To really embrace our making lives, we have to be brave enough to maybe make something that will be wildly ugly. When the flurry of the making is done, the creative rush is over, we have to look at the thing we made.

Yep—Look. I made that. And it might be lovely. And it might not.

On a good day, this is a wonder of a way to live. I walk by my sheet-and-chenille-covered recliner and think: *Dangit I love that thing. I made it.* And I sort of mentally high five myself out of satisfaction.

But then there are those other days when the clouds are inside instead of outside, the days where my dark heart just seems to be scanning around crazily for proof that I'm the screw-up I fear that I am. All I can see everywhere I look are wobbly seams. It all looks a little too homemade.

When days like these come around, the things I've made seem almost embarrassing to me. Like little kids in fancy dresses with unbrushed hair: dear—but vulnerable in their beauty. And I feel a little exposed to the world. And in those moments, I often want to throw away some of what I've made. Get it out of my sight.

Because making something opens us up to the possibility that we are not the amazing maker we wish we were. My heart braces itself regularly for some guy in a suit to come to the door and tell me that I am no longer allowed to make things. "Your license has been revoked," he'll say,

"You're stuff's too ugly." Or something like that. And I'll go search in my wallet—and, you know, give him my Makers License. (SINCE THOSE EXIST.)

So I get it if you're nervous to make things. I get it if you've been putting off allotting more of your time to making things. I get it if the things that other people would call excuses feel a whole lot more like really good reasons to you.

But I say, let's not settle for being creative chickens, always out to protect our I'm Not All That Bad A Maker status. Let's push past it. Let's get good at looking at the mediocre stuff we make and seeing it for what it all is: just some mediocre stuff, stuff that can be remade or thrown out and tried again.

The more things I make, the better I get at playing through these small failures. When my hands are moving, I can hear deeper voices, truer voices, the ones that remind me that I'm not the stuff I make: I'm me. It's the making that's given me confidence to keep at it when those ghosts-in-suits show up.

I couldn't live with myself if I didn't tell you the whole truth: I think we don't make things because we are afraid. And I thought you should know that I'm afraid sometimes too, and that making stuff anyway has made me more brave—the best kind of brave I could be: brave enough to believe that the things I make don't say a bit about the right I have to keep making them.

They're just things I make. And I really like to make them. And I really think that down deep in there you do too.

HOW TO READ THIS BOOK

Don't just read this book. Honestly, the worst thing that could ever happen to you (okay, in my world) would be that you'd read this book and then get to the end and NOTHING WOULD BE DIFFERENT FOR YOU. That would be serious bad news.

You don't need more inspiration, friend. You need a new way to go forward.

So, I've included a boatload of thinking-with-your-hands kinds of exercises. If you do them, by the end you will have shaken up your own head a bit.

They'll be tempting to skip. But don't. Reading about new ideas is always nice, but if you really want to uncover your own stuck spots, give them a shot.

Sometimes writing is the very best way to see our own heads more clearly. When we write, it's like being able to shake off the ropes—we start to bounce above those stuck places, like thinking inside of a room filled with trampolines.

This kind of writing-to-think works best done quickly and without a lot of worry about how it all might look or sound to somebody else. So please consider the questions in these chapters, but don't lie on the couch and stare off into space about them. Write about them. Talk to yourself with a pen. When you don't know what to write, write down, "I don't know what to write" or "Ginger is lame" or "I need to do the freaking dishes, so why am I sitting here writing about my duck carving life?" Just write down something. This sort of writing will start to shine a big box full of flashlights on the corners of your own brain that you'd otherwise be squinting to see.

(WRITE) and (DRAW) ideas are included throughout for just this sort of thinking on paper.

Don't make a big deal about this. Please do not drive to an expensive bookstore and buy a book covered in leather. It won't work. Trust me. You'll be wasting time in the car, and then when you get the thing home you'll just feel like you need to jot down ideas that are worthy of being covered in leather. These are not the sorts of ideas you need to capture.

You need the freedom to jot down cheap thoughts. A cheap book will help you pull this off.

If you don't have a cheap composition book lying around your house or in the bottom of some weird drawer full of school supplies, go to the drugstore and get yourself one. I like to use the one dollar composition books with the black and white covers. (You can even get them with blank pages or with graph paper. Pick whatever makes you happy.)

Get a pen you really like, too. And then clip it to the cheap composition book and don't use it to write checks with or anything nasty like that. Leave it stuck to your book so it's there all undefiled and ready to go.

(go do this) pages will give you some activities to try. They're intended to stretch your believing around the places where you may be stuck in your making life. I'll tell you straight out: you're going to think they're goofy. You'll likely want to just read them and tell somebody about what good ideas they are…but never do them.

I think you ought to do them.

A really wise person told me—okay, it was my therapist— that we often think we can fix everything in our heads, that we can think our way out of our stuck places. But it doesn't always work that way. Our hands have more help to give our insides than we'd guess. She said this all much more eloquently, of course, but you get the idea.

Don't stay stuck. Stop waiting.

It really is possible to have the making life that you wish you did. And much sooner than you'd think.

INTRODUCTION:
WE'RE ALL MEANT TO MAKE

I don't think I was made to be a buyer of things. A judge of things. An organizer of things. A deliverer of things or people. Or at least not only.

And I don't think you were either. I think we're meant to be makers—built to build.

Part of me wants to say that you believe this too. That I don't have to really talk you into it. That if you were left alone long enough to just try at something you like doing, you'd easily nod your head when I said to you, "you're supposed to be making things!" That if you noticed you were criticizing yourself for the final product and how the glue was going to show, you'd likely see how messed up that sort of self-talk is—and how common. That if you practiced doing this enough times, you might hear your own soul whispering that it was actually having a good time. And you might be willing to do it again.

This peace isn't just supposed to be available for "talented" people or "artists." We're all made to do this stuff.

The steady-hearted place that comes with making seems to grow a thing that feels spiritual, God-reaching, something like what prayer is likely meant to be: our souls still, our hands moving, the hamsters that usually ride stationary bikes in our heads strangely calmed (sipping water on the sidelines somewhere). And this experience is a vastly more important thing to foster and make space for than the product of our quilts or bags or hand-cut invitations would lead anybody on the outside of our souls to believe.

When we sew or glue or carve or bake, we're doing a sort of little play, a one-act, of the way we know life is meant to be. We're taking pieces and turning them into something—making things whole.

We are sitting still with our soul and doing something that we all want to see everywhere we look: watching a thing turn into something. We are surrounded by pieces. We want to be surrounded by whole things. And when we make, we enact this. We affirm for ourselves and our own hearts that while broken pieces, scattered bits, fragments, shards, are what it often feels that our lives are made of, whole things, finished beauties, these are the things that we know we're made to be surrounded by, what our hearts are hankering for.

And the enactment of that play at the sewing table or drawing table or carving table sends messages to our hearts that don't arrive in platitudes or even measurable quantities. I think they arrive in some neuron-version of a big plate of hot cheese potatoes. Like food. Like comfort. Like warmth. Like a little of what we need. And our souls sit down and take off their shoes. And they eat. And they feel full.

And this peace isn't just supposed to be available to some people—not just for "talented" people or "artists." We're all made to do this stuff.

We're all meant to make. Because of the way modern culture has evolved with all its factories and long conveyor belts pumping out the things that our hands were meant to give us, we've been robbed of one of the big pieces of our daily life: making things.

What if a stiller version of our days lies before us and we never reach out to grab it?

The fact that my house is scattered with handmade rag rugs surely makes the place feel more like home, but it's the stillness I find in the making that makes me a kinder, calmer person in it. The impact to my heart from the activity of making completely outshines the beauty of even the loveliest thing I've ever created.

For those of us with jumpy insides, it's nice to find a way

to keep some parts of our bodies moving while our souls still. That's worth finding time for. It's worth stopping everything, hucking off our own strange willingness to care more about not wanting to screw up than we do about the happiness of our own made-to-make souls. Totally worth it.

And we don't need a bit of talent to claim it.

GET A PEN. HERE WE GO.

HOW DO YOU HAVE TIME
FOR ALL THAT?

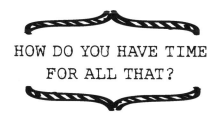

HOW DO YOU HAVE TIME
FOR ALL THAT?

I get this a lot.

Like I'm standing at the punch bowl at some relative's wedding, and I say to somebody who makes even a flicker of eye contact with me, "Want to talk about my new hobby of sewing for the next 45 minutes, wherein I will give you six reasons for loving old polyester and draw a map of local thrift stores on a cocktail napkin?" They generally nod and glance over my shoulder for somebody else they know at the party. And then they say in response to my well-intended, completely impassioned rant about the Importance of Making in Our Lives: "How do you have time for all that?"

And I'm wondering who else out there is hearing it, and I'm also wondering if anybody's responding with anything real.

I mean, there's…

"Well, I MAKE time, because I believe my creative life is important."

I don't know how anybody else is managing to do their kid life and their relationship life and their work life and their self life without their creative life.

But then I sound like a Lady Prick. And nobody likes an LP.

"Well, I never do the dishes, my kids haven't had haircuts, and I recently found the baby swishing around a thumb tack in her little mouth. Oh. And I don't volunteer in the kids' classroom."

But then I sound like Slacker Lady. And everybody talks about SL when they go out to coffee before their volunteering.

"Well, my husband pitches in a lot with the kids—and around the house." To which they look sideways at me and either ask or think, "He's not annoyed that you're always SEWING?"

But then I sound like She's Got a Perfect Husband Lady.

And everybody really hates SGPHL because they think of her house like the Lido Deck of the Love Boat of Living.

The real tension here, though—beyond not wanting to sound prickish or slackery or overly-taken-care-of is that I really don't know how anybody else doesn't have enough time. And by that I mean Time. I don't know how anybody else is managing to do their Kid Life and their Relationship Life and their Work Life and their Self Life without their Creative Life.

And I really don't understand how our culture has sold us that the list is supposed to go:

1. Kid Life
2. Work Life
3. Spouse Life
4. Self Life
5. Creative Life

Or maybe if you're Oprah or the President of ebay or an ambassador to an emerging country, #4 goes first, followed in a dead heat by #2 and you may or may not skip #1 and #3.

But why is our creative life a luxury? The more I make, the more I believe that it's not a luxury. It's a life means. I would even say it's a lifeboat means. It keeps me bobbing when a lot of the other stuff looks like wreckage.

I think we're supposed to figure these tensions out, and not run away from them—not from the people at parties who keep asking us with semi-judgmental looks on their faces, and not from ourselves either.

YOU LOVE TO MAKE THINGS,
BUT YOU DON'T

Let's talk honestly about this. You love to make things. When you sit and sew/keep bees/crochet/paste, your soul starts walking a little more slowly. You notice that you breathe differently. There is a quiet inside of you that mixes with a little buzz of energy that makes a cocktail in your heart that feels just exactly how you'd like to be in the world all of the time.

And when you tell people that you make things, they say, "What do you make?" and then you think to yourself, *my button earring project sounds mega-lame*...so you say, "earrings." And then they say, "Do you sell them?" and then you say, "Um. No. I just give them as gifts."

Just.

And then some time goes by. You don't make button earrings for a while. And you find that you're really agitated.

Two months later you're cleaning the upstairs and you come across the buttons and the glue and all that other stuff. And you sit down with your bucket of cleaning supplies ditched right next to you, and you just start making another pair right there on the floor in front of the closet. You're wearing house-cleaning pants. Your hair isn't washed. You're supposed to be somewhere in 45 minutes. But you just start gluing, and then you make another pair. You spread the dirty dust rags out around you and lay the button earrings on them to dry. And then there are seven pair, and you're digging in the button jar for a match to the next one you want to use when you look at your watch and you realize that you're late. You jump up—your hips hurt and maybe your foot is asleep—and you grab a hat because you were going to take a shower before you got in the car, but you are out of time. And as you drive in the car to get your dog from the groomer or your kid from tap class, you realize you're just a little happier, more contented inside.

And it's not because your button earrings will sell 32 pairs a day on etsy. And it's not because anybody came by and said, "ooohhh those are so pretty." It's because you made something. And that's what making feels like: soul-settling.

And you could use some more of that, right?

Yes. I thought so.

You love to make things, but you don't. Because sometimes your head just goes south about the whole thing and all that inner clatter of voices telling you that you're not talented and that you could never sell any of it anyway is just too much. It's easier to just wait and tell yourself you'll have time for that sort of thing later in your life …

I know.

But it doesn't have to be like that. You can love to make things. Even if you're sure you're no good at it. Even if you have no time or no money or your closet is already full of weird polyester baby dresses you could never get anybody to buy at the craft fair that one time.

`You don't have to always be wishing that you could squeeze in time for the thing that makes your heart the happiest.`

What if it was okay that you didn't sell anything you make? What if you let yourself get to it before you've a) cleaned the house b) done the taxes c) finished studying or d) "caught up."

It might be that the things you're telling yourself aren't as true as they sound. And it might be that you could see them differently and find the space and time and freedom that you need. And it might be that you'd start to make more things.

And that would be fantastic.

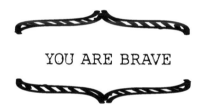

YOU ARE BRAVE

L et's be perfectly clear here: I'm not naturally brave. I'm naturally a lot of things (a nervous helper, an often-inappropriate clown-head, a person who runs into door jambs): but I'm not naturally brave. I think the cave people my line descended from ran out at night for nuts and then hid all day. That's my best anthropological guess about the backstory of my DNA.

Bravery: hard; Hiding: easy.

I have not broken my leg doing anything.

I would not saw off my arm if it were stuck in between two rocks. (I think I'd more likely write a really long journal entry on one of the rocks with paste concocted from dirt and spit.)

I'm sure there are snakes everywhere trying to bite me.

I'm petrified of the TSA.

I have collected little chicken figurines for years and only recently seen how pathetically metaphoric this is about me. And how true.

Truth is, I'm afraid a lot of the time.

But I recently quit a job that my soul had really suffered with for more than half of the fifteen years I stayed at it. I walked away from steady income and a reasonably legit thing to tell people I did and headed straight out toward God Knows What.

And that wasn't the really brave thing I did, actually. The brave thing happened five years ago.

I made a potholder. And it was the bravest thing I've ever done.

I was walking around a vacation town on a weekend away with some girlfriends and we were in the 44th store selling all matter of goods with words stamped on them. I'd finally had it. "I need a pillow that says something besides DELICIOUS HAPPINESS or EFFERVESCENT DELIRIUM or HAPPY HOME on it. Why doesn't anyone make a pillow that says SWEATY FEET or SOMETIMES PRETTY GOOD or WE MOSTLY LOVE EACH OTHER MOST DAYS? And then I ranted on like this for a while to I think the last of my three friends who'd started into the store with me. And then a book caught my eye—it was a beginner's sewing book. I picked it up, saw an easy-to-make pattern for a potholder, bought the thing and immediately knew I would make the easy-to-sew potholder, most importantly stamped with these words: IT'S NOT BURNED IT'S CRISPY LIKE WE LIKE IT.

This was actually a radical decision. I hate to screw up. I don't call myself a perfectionist: I'm just a person who would rather succeed than fail and also abhors the idea of other people seeing me screw up especially if I was trying really hard to do a good job and prefers it when things turn out the way that I imagine that they should.

So, yeah. Do you have this too? Sorry—too personal. You probably aren't a perfectionist either. You're probably just somebody who likes it when the things you make turn out perfectly.

I get the difference. I really do.

Making the potholder that I didn't know how to make wasn't the sort of move I generally made in my life. I didn't exactly know how to sew. I have plenty of things I can do well, things I've organized my entire personality around, so doing something I knew I'd suck at was actually a bold move.

I set about to make it, made it, and it turned out ugly. The cute little edging was all wobbly looking. Also I bought the wrong weight of inside lining so I burned my hand when I used it.

And then the even bolder move I made was that after the potholder turned out sort of lame, I made something else. And then I just kept making things—about 30 aprons, a couch cover out of old polyester, stacks of retro baby dresses, piles of purses, and lots of weird curtains from old sheets.

So when friends say things to me like, "If I buy a headboard cover made out of ugly fabric, will you take the $200 worth of gorgeous linen that I'll buy at a remnant shop and make a new cover for it?"

I say: "Sure."

> Why do we feel like we need to know what we're doing in order to do it?

Is this because I am an expert? Nope. It's because I'm willing to dive into the deep end without thought for what ugliness might emerge. Frankly, I'm so taken with the possibility that something fantastic could come of my sewing together fabric that would otherwise be trash, that I don't give fear of my own potential failure any thought. Plus, my best projects have emerged from projects that I had to think and re-think and rip out and then re-think again.

After years of regular sewing and making from fabric I rescue from thrift shops and yard sales and the backs of people's closets, I've never become shockingly, amazingly skilled at any of it. I use my seam ripper as often as I use my machine. I regularly botch zippers (I mean, they work, but the ends of them are not State Fair material), and my eyes roll into the back of my head and the room swirls around a little when anybody talks about warp and weft. (Terms make me queasy.) I rarely know how much trouble the project will be until I'm up to my elbows in it. I rarely know, because it doesn't occur to me to care. This is, of course, why I'm rarely afraid to try.

Most often, I don't know what I'm even doing until I'm part way through it. In fact, sometimes when I make something it's like trying to follow bad directions somebody scribbled on a napkin: I go for a while and then inevitably find myself in some unexpected cul de sac and have to turn around, retrace some steps, try another way. I always arrive somewhere by a much more interesting means than I expected to.

And now I hear a lot of *You are Brave*.

This is funny to me because I'm often standing in front of a huge bucket of thrift store fabric, holding a little pair of scissors and covered in thread. I feel sure I don't look the picture of bravery. Not valiant, not powerfully willing to take on pain. The words "nerdy" and "quilter" come to mind, actually—and these words don't conjure up bravery for me as much as they make me worried I will end up carrying a patchwork purse before I'm 50.

But brave is the word they use. Over and over again.

And it's made me see how afraid everybody around me is to make anything.

(Like a cloth napkin, even.)

Why do we feel like we need to know what we're doing in order to do it? What are we afraid of? What can go wrong? I'm not yelling this. I'm leaning in across a small table at a coffee shop, asking you: *What can go wrong? Why do you need to have it all figured out before you dive in?*

WONKAPHOBIA

Sometimes we do claim the time. We claim the space. We pull out the little stash of supplies we've squirreled away at the back of a closet somewhere for ourselves.

Everybody's gone. The house is quiet. We pull out the sewing machine. Or the crochet hooks. Or the book about how to keep bees or make paper mache. We dive in with our whole soul and make something. We lose time to it. We forget to eat. We pop our heads up and notice it got dark outside when we weren't looking.

We've finished what we were making. And it doesn't look like what we thought it was going to.

It looks, well, wonky. Off just a bit.

And we say: *Guy. That doesn't look right. I must not be good at this.*

We decide we better use clearer instructions next time. We buy books. We scour blogs for well-written tutorials with lots of pictures. We stare for hours online at pictures of things that other people made…things where none of the dried glue ever shows.

We find another day. We stare at the pictures in the book or on the website where everybody who already knows how to do what we're trying to do swears that it's not that hard, actually. We thread and re-thread and re-thread our machines. We cast on and off and on and off and on and off. We stand really still and wait for the bees to come. We make the newspaper goop with great care and less water.

But then even this strained instruction-following doesn't work. None of it is what we thought it would be. The toaster cover we're sewing is too small. The dog sweater we're knitting is too big. The bees are apparently living at the neighbor's house. And the paper mache bell pepper still looks more like an unripe tomato.

We say it again: *I must not be good at this.*

And then we set aside the one we made and go buy a factory-made version that looks more like the one we had envisioned when we sat down in the first place.

There are things to say here about how expensive this can all become: how we pay double—for the supplies we purchased to make the one we wanted + the cheap one that we bought.

But wait: it's worse. We pay even more. We pay the cost of that all-wrong message ping-ponging around in our heads looking for a place to land and stay: I must not be good at this.

Forget the $36 worth of fabric or yarn or hive colony cases. It's the cost of that message that's really the price.

And usually what happens is that it stops us up for a while. We hold off on our project-ing. We buy what we want. We read about projects but don't do them. We go to handmade craft fairs and buy things. But we don't really make for a while. Then enough time goes by, or maybe that urge in us to just make something becomes so strong that we can't ignore it.

And this time when we sit down, something has shifted. We're no longer just making something that we want. Now we're doing something even trickier: we're trying to make something to prove that the other message we've started believing isn't real.

The pressure is on. Our teeth are sort of clenched while we're at the work table. If we glanced in a mirror, there's a chance we'd be frowning.

We're trying to make a perfect thing—something that has no wonk, something that will yell *You are good at this* loudly enough that we'll believe it.

Sometimes when we sit down to make something, we're doing a lot more than we know we are. We think we're sewing a shirt, but we're really trying to prove something. When we weren't looking, we started trying to do something much more complicated: we're trying to believe we are actually good at what we want to be good at doing. Usually we're trying to emulate a perfect, wonk-free machine to pull this off.

This is too bad. Because regular people don't make perfect things. They make handmade things—and handmade things regularly have some sort of proof around them that gives the person who owns it a little hint that it was made by a human.

Many of us call this "wonk."

And it's nothing we ought to be afraid of.

We need to make friends with wonk—invite it to tea. Serve it biscuits. Ask it about its childhood. Consider its finer points and stop judging its obvious irregularities. Because when wonk is present, it's a sign that an actual human has constructed the thing we're looking at. Wonk indicates humanity.

In the things that we make ourselves for our homes and our families, wonk just means that we didn't walk into a store to meet our own needs. And it probably means that we or whoever made the thing experienced something in the making: joy, relaxation, the-frustration-of-trying-something-never-before-tried, even creative triumph.

Wonk means something happened for somebody.

We change the world a little when we declare that we are a human and not a factory. Maybe when we make something that a human would make, more and more people will start to understand that useable, beautiful objects don't always have perfectly straight lines. And that those things aren't broken; they're just made by somebody's actual hands.

Wonk is lovely: it's not an indicator of lack of expertise or failure. It's just a sign that a person made it.

What if we opened up our arms wide to the possibility that what we make might look wonky? It's true that we'd probably make some real doozers—some stuff that would cause people to turn their heads away and make uncomfortable eye contact with one another outside of our gaze. Stuff that a mother would have to concentrate to love.

> Wonk is lovely: it's not an indicator of lack of expertise or failure. It's just a sign that a person made it.

But then after we did this a few or twenty times, something would shift. We'd get better at making prom dresses. The seams would be straighter, and we'd learn how to more deftly glue on the plastic flowers that covered the snaps at the waist. Our thin straps would be thinner...and less bumpy, our hand-stitched hemlines smoother.

If we did this long enough, we might find that when we walked into the gym—some day, like maybe eight proms from now—some people would stare in a different way. They'd stare out of interest.

Because they'd be seeing something that hadn't been done before. *White Eyelet with hot pink polyester accents? Oooohhhh.*

It can turn out that a willingness to produce an ugly thing transforms itself an ability to produce a beautiful thing, a thing that would otherwise not happen.

In the meantime, isn't it a kindness to make a humble object? Think of what we are telling our friends when we give them something that has a sweet, little flaw. Think of the possibilities we've declared to them with our own public willingness to be just good enough and thoroughly well intentioned in our giving. Think of how relieved they will be that we didn't put all of our energy into showing off—that we put a whole lot more of it into thinking of them while we sculpted their first initial out of a bar of soap.

It actually adds up to something better than either making or handing over a thing that is entirely wonk-free, a thing with square edges and orderly seams. Those things land at a friend's house and might tell her with their squareness and well-measuredness that the other things in her house should look the same.

Think of how your friend might think, "Hey: I could do that." And how she won't look at your gift when the party's over and think, "She's so good at that. Geez. I could never do that." *postpartyslump*

Every time we make a thing that lets a little wonk into the world, we make space for a little more.

MORE GUTS AND LESS NERVOUSNESS

I'm not saying that learning to sew cured all my fears. It didn't. (Try flying with me some time—my friends walk me to straight to the Gin Dispenser in the airport if we have more than 20 minutes between flights.)

I've been chipping away at them for years with, you know: twenty years of therapy, a flagrantly spastic and deeply committed spiritual life, a small circle of friends who nod when I talk and never walk away, a husband who laughs when I become so emotionally complex that I am no longer a rationally functioning human.

And I also sometimes walk upstairs and just start cutting up weird old fabric with only a slightly more specific plan than the one I had when I stopped taking birth control pills—a sort of Hey That's Probably Going to Be a Good Idea I'll Figure It Out sort of take on creating something. And that habit has helped a lot.

As it turns out, whatever we commit our hands to over and over, well, our hearts are paying really close attention too.

We get good at whatever we practice—we know this is true of tennis and calf roping, but we might be less apt to believe it about our souls. And when our souls practice requiring every last thing around us to be perfect, well, then we get really good at that.

In the same way, if we let our souls practice seeing things fall just a little short of where we imagined they could be, then our souls will get better at that. And feeling comfortable in the midst of imperfection is a beautiful skill to master. Without it, we're easily led to believe that the sight of the imperfection is somehow a sign that we're really just meant to be doing something else.

But it's not. When things are imperfect, it's usually because they're either just not finished (even if they're imperfect at the moment when the maker expected them to be finished). Or sometimes it's possible that they're considered imperfect because the person looking at them has sort of, well, unrealistic standards. Also, too, there's always just the chance that they just are—imperfect, I mean.

Imperfection may be true of a thing; it doesn't say a bit about the thing-maker.

When I am stuck in my creative life, I lean in and look at what I'm doing, then do something different. I live with the surety that the problem I'm facing is just that—a problem, and not a sign, not a message from heaven or anywhere else that I'm not meant to be doing what I'm doing. I imagine some would call this confidence. But read slowly enough here to take in that the confidence I've found has come as a byproduct of being sure that if I'm no good at whatever my hands are doing, nothing bad is going to happen to me. Nobody will take my scissors and old upholstery fabric away from me and tell me to give up and go home.

It will mean maybe that I make some ugly stuff that I throw away or give away later, but none of it will ever kick me out of the sandbox.

Really, if we are not enjoying the process of our making—the idea-having, piece-cutting, problem-solving, sewing-it-all-up and then tearing-it-apart-because-it's-not-quite-right-yet process—as much as we're loving what we end up with when we're finished with a project, well, then, we're just flat out missing the boat.

And also, if we're not willing to live on the edge a little and dive into a project that might not turn out perfectly, well then we're missing another boat there too.

I don't think we're all crazy to assume that only really talented people are the ones who spend their lives making things. Everywhere we look, there's a book promising us all the tricks of whatever trade we're dreaming about. And on a good day, those books can be really encouraging. They can give us the sort of boost we need to tackle what we want to.

But they often send us another message too—something about how everybody else must know more than we do…And that if we just knew more, we'd be able to make all the things we ever wanted to.

> It's not more information that we need to get us rolling. We need more fearlessness, more unbridled willingness to try.

I say that's a bunch of bupkus.

I was once asked to review a book on sewing for my blog that would've given me every last bit of information about the technical aspects of sewing. But this is all I could think of while I was reading through the (very thorough) sewing book: we don't need any more information.

We just need more guts and less nervousness and more surety that nothing bad will happen if we just tuck in and try.

I really don't think anybody out there is rightfully confused. And hold on, here's how I mean it: there are plenty of resources (many, many of them completely free now) that will help us figure out the snazzier tricks. And there are many friendly guides for getting started at anything we'd like to begin trying our hands at—whatever gluing, carving, sculpting, macrameing activity we want to tackle.

It's not more information that we need to get us rolling. We need more fearlessness, more unbridled willingness to try. Because when we do jump in and just try, we figure out all of the things that the lady in the book has tried and figured out and is showing us . . . so that we won't have to try to figure it all out for ourselves.

But figuring it all out for ourselves is the best part.

Many of us are so white knuckled to our own perfectionism that we're missing out. On the best part.

Don't miss out. Be willing to figure it out.

This blind boldness—this willingness to make something that may be really tragic looking or may be wonderful, coupled with the belief that potential wrong turns will just be chances to solve more problems—has helped me well beyond my growing talent for turning old polyester into useful household objects.

You don't have to go sew to become brave. But I'm not going to lie: I think you ought to give it a shot. Practice making something. Practice making something that might look fantastically Lame.

Don't think of it as making something: think of it as practice—practice at being brave. Because if we can embrace a way of practicing being boldly unafraid in our creative lives, then maybe we'll become braver at other things, right?

GOOD JOB STAYING WITH ME. NOW WE'RE GETTING TO THE NITTY GRITTY.

GET
UNSTUCK

GET UNSTUCK

Maybe if we understood bravery differently, we'd all have a better shot at being brave.

We easily imagine brave people to be those who know they will die or be maimed, riding valiantly forward (usually on a horse) to face what they know is ahead.

But I don't think that is the best picture of bravery—it's at least not one that helps us much.

I don't think bravery is always about facing horrific ends—sometimes being brave means moving forward in the face of horrific possibilities that also might bring beautiful ends. It means accepting the fact that all might not go the way we'd like it to—and that reality is the cost of the possibility that it actually might turn out just the way we've imagined. But we won't know. And still we have to go.

When fear is in charge, our feet refuse to understand this. They just don't go. We're stuck. Powerful fear doesn't always make us run away: sometimes it just makes us freeze. If we just don't move forward, that means, maybe nothing bad will happen. Somewhere down deep we see that nothing good will happen either if we stay put, but we're willing to pay the price. We stay paralyzed in a kind of fantasy that not moving will keep us from all bad ends.

This, of course, means that we are regularly stuck—planted in place, sure that moving forward will result in an untimely experience of something horrific. Paralysis becomes the way we control our lives.

And sure, this is all easy to understand when the picture is of a guy on a horse and the dragon is there on top of the hill and he's got to decide what to do. If we had a bullhorn, we'd likely yell something at him like, "DON'T JUST STAND THERE!"

But it's harder to see in ourselves around things like our creative lives. We don't think of the ugly purse we might make with expensive material as the equivalent of a fire-breathing dragon, but our feet make the connection: they see that we might spend a lot of time doing something that in the end we have to hear some mean voice in our head say "That's Lame." And because our souls really, really don't like hearing things like that, they just sort of freeze.

If our nervous-to-fail insides have us in full-blown paralysis in our creative lives, we're missing the mark. I just know we are. We're not actually succeeding in any way that our souls were made to…We're just a Not Failure.

We need a different goal than perfectionism—because stuckness is a sad, dark place.

Are you maybe stuck?

You know you love to make things—today it's a fall wreath out of pinecones and old thread spools. You saw a picture of this somewhere. You were considering whipping all the thread off all the spools you've got, but it seems wasteful. So you're going to wait until all the thread is used from your entire stash and do this next fall.

You've got ideas of the things you want to make—and friends who actually do these things and don't only think about them. But weeks go by—months even—where you never give attention to the part of your soul that wants to make things.

You've even got supplies for the things you like to make stashed somewhere—not in an easy-to-get to spot, likely— but somewhere. And you own lots of books about making the things you love to make. And you read blogs where other people make the sorts of things you like to make. You wish you were better at it—better at doing whatever it is you love to do.

And you believe in your heart that there will be a time when it won't be like this: some day you will be better at it because you'll have more time and more space.

You might remember back to a time when your making life was more full. And you feel like some day it will be again. It's agitating that it's not right now, but what could you do about it?

Don't wait. Time's not gonna fix it. I swear. I really wish it would, but I don't think it will.

I suspect that there are things you're telling yourself that are holding you back from throwing yourself at your creative life. I suspect that the reasons you're using sound true. And I want to tell you that they are legitimate reasons, surely . . . but I also think that there's a chance that you've swallowed some other truth about yourself as a creative person that are likely a bunch of bunk.

What if you could see past those excuses that your brain keeps shoveling at you to keep you from sitting down and just making something for fun? Maybe if you could see the message for its dark underbelly, you'd know how to kick it off your porch and walk forward . . . right over to the card table where you have all your wood burning tools just sitting, waiting, covered in dust.

The truth is, I don't think you're out of time or talent or money or any of that, I think you might be just stuck. Have you talked yourself into believing a bunch of lies about what it means to be a creative person? I think those thoughts are getting in the way of your living a way better life.

And I don't mean here that by taking time to scrapbook or knit you're going to solve all of your problems and not have to breathe through your nose a lot of the time just to get through a given day.

But I do mean this: some of your days could be better. A lot better. And if you had enough of those days add up, they could turn into weeks. And before you knew it, a lot of what you called your "life" would look more like what you used to hope it would look like.

I say: lean in; get unstuck.

I DON'T HAVE TIME

When I'm upstairs surrounded by mounds of old polyester, and I've got 18 minutes before my ride's going to pick me up to go visit my sister, and I know I want something to tote my laptop in, and I'm racing the clock and combining colors and stitching at the speed of light . . . it feels the same as it did when I was riding my bike with no hands down the street toward my friend Maureen's house. Full. And Happy. And Exhilarating even.

Other times, though, it is hard for me to feel like I can lean in to my creative life before I finish the "work."

Some days the dirty dishes in my sink are actually doing more to my life than just stinking the place up. They're actually a little picture that is communicating to me about what it means for me to "accomplish" enough in my life. They are saying to me: "To the extent that I'm still in here, you're still not working." You have more work to do. On good days, I can walk right by a fat stack of dishes and not even blink. This is not because I have low sanitary standards: it's because I've started to practice thinking differently about the immediacy of "work" and how sometimes it shoves out the stuff we sideline because we call it "play."

Many of us who live with an ache in our souls to make something—to sew something, carve something, glue something, write something, sing something, dance something, weave something—tell ourselves that if we're grown-ups, then we'll do these things once the accounting and coordinating and house-grime-management and schlepping and volunteer board meetings are over.

We'll play once the work is done.

Sure, sometimes our lives have to be that way. I haven't met a single infant who's understood my need for a full creative life. Not a one of them stopped crying to make space for me. Sometimes we have seasons within our working lives that are so physically exhausting (either from the heavy physical lifting or sometimes from heavy emotional or intellectual lifting) that the thought of leaning toward moments of creativity just doesn't sound fun. We're just flat out too tired. Sometimes we have to take more shifts at work and the math about only being alive 24 hours a day doesn't even make sense. Sometimes we really don't have any time.

But I feel sure that our lives are not as busy as we say they are. I don't think that our schedules are the primary thing keeping us from what we want. I think, instead, that it has a lot more to do with the way that we separate "work" and "play" in our thinking—and specifically the idea that in order to be reasonable grown-ups, we ought to be completely finished with the one before we give ourselves the freedom to tackle the other.

What I've noticed about this sort of body/brain split is that it's led me to do both things—the sort of things I've always considered "work" (cleaning up in the house, grading papers, paying the bills, cooking dinner) as well as the sorts of things I've considered "play" (sewing, crocheting, writing and gluing)—well, not very well.

I've needed to solve the problem of my constant state of wanting to be somewhere that I'm not. So, I've finally thrown my hands up in the air and accepted the reality that it doesn't work for me to split my life into work and play.

The starkest reality for me is that I've never once as a teacher/writer / mother-of-three / active non-profit volunteer come to a single hour where the "work" was complete. Never once. And so when I've lived with this sort of way of thinking about my creative life, I've either gone for long, long periods of time without any single creative outlet, or I've made a point to get the time for myself and then felt sort of bad about it—like I'm playing hooky from my real life, and like I should write an apology note to somebody about it.

The highest impact move I've made to combat this tension has been to pull my creative life under the traditional category of "work" in my own head. If I can re-define "work" to mean "the sorts of things that I think are meaningful for how I want to live" rather than "the stuff I want to get over with" or "the stuff I make money doing," well then it's a win-win for me. I've upgraded my sense of how I want to be in my world, and I've made space for a better version of myself while I'm doing all of those things.

I started by declaring that making is important. I started saying things like, "Everybody thinks of our creative lives as the mashed potatoes, but it's the meat. It's central. Important." I started going upstairs as a regular part of my week. I didn't wait for the work to be over. I claimed it as necessary and real and part of what I needed to do to live how I wanted to live. I just required that my regular life included it.

This was tricky, of course. When I first made this move, some nights I was using my newly-claimed conviction that I wanted to live a maker's life as a smokescreen for the reality that I was just in a bad mood. Other nights, though, I really wasn't. Other nights I was climbing the stairs as a proclamation of how I want to live—and I knew that if I didn't just jump in and start including it all, that there would be no space made for it. Essentially I began by acting as if I knew it were true.

I made a space for myself that just wasn't there before. My family understands now that making is some of what I do to be me. They don't wonder about it. They don't experience it as a threat or an escape. They know I really like to make things. They think my going upstairs sometimes to sew or crochet or cut up old game boards is a perfectly normal thing to do.

(WRITE)

GRUMPINESS INVENTORY

Go fold a piece of paper in half long ways so you've got a couple of good-looking columns. At the top of one half write WORK and on the other half, write PLAY. Now fill them in. Write nice and fast so you don't try to put down the "right answer"—just jot down what's true right now. What sorts of activities do you consider "work" and which do you consider "play"? Next, draw a schedule of a typical week for you. Fill it in with the activities you've listed above—and be sure to label the time "work" and "play."

Now do a Grumpiness Inventory. Mark on your schedule page which times you tend to find yourself feeling free and ready to be alive and which parts of the day you tend to be a grumpy piece of work. Finally, stare at the page and look for insight...What's your "work" to "play" ratio? Are there any patterns to your grumpiness? Are there windows to increase the amount of making in your life?

(You might want to use this blank space or maybe the lines on the next page to make that work & play list. Or you might want to write your grocery list here since it is distracting you while you are trying to get your thoughts dumped. You can do whatever you want to—but go write that grumpiness inventory somewhere. On an old napkin that you can burn later if you want to. Just write it somewhere.)

(go do this)

DIRTY DISHES DANCING

Try mixing work and play. Dance in your kitchen. I don't mean this metaphorically. I am not suggesting that you live in a way that a country song implies that you really ought to live. I mean it literally: dance in your kitchen. If you can manage to have a sink full of dirty dishes waiting to be washed, well then all the better. If you don't know how to dance, then just pretend to dance: pretend you're Beyonce or John Travolta or Napoleon Dynamite. Pick somebody who you've seen dance and just pretend to be them for a bit. Loud music will help you with this. Try saying something to all the people in your house like, "Um. I'm going to do some extensive mopping with a new special cleaning solution that will melt your shoes, so I need to be here alone and wear a special mask. Come back in an hour." Go to whatever fancy radio you use that lets you tell them what to play. Select one of these stations: A) The Bee Gees B) Earth Wind & Fire C) Whatever-you-loved-to-listen-to-in-high-school. Turn it on. Dance. Stare at the dirty dishes. Keep dancing.

Write the name of the song you danced to right here so that you don't forget and so that in three years when you pick this book back up again you can play the song and dance to it all over again and it will all sink in even deeper.

....

....

....

DO YOU SEE HOW THIS IS GOING TO GO?
I'M GOING TO GIVE YOU THESE CHANCES TO
LEAN IN AND TRY WRITING ABOUT WHAT'S UP
WITH YOU. SOMETIMES THEY WILL SEEM LIKE
GOOD IDEAS AND OTHER TIMES YOU WILL WANT
TO SKIP THEM. BUT DON'T, OKAY? THEY'LL HELP.
I SWEAR.

I'M TOO TIRED

Y ou're really tired. And I know the kind of tired you might be too—the bad kind of tired.

There is the kind of tired that comes with painting your bedroom all weekend long and eating nothing but top ramen at 11 at night because you are so driven to get the thing done. And then when you're finished, you sit on your bed (once all that plastic is thrown away) and your muscles ache, and you think, "Better."

But then there's that other kind of tired: where you sit in your car and look out at something and don't really see it.

The foggy kind, the kind where you feel a little lost most of the time. Where a lot of the time you walk into a room and can't remember why you went there.

That's the bad kind of tired. It feels more like disorientation than it does sleepiness. And that, I believe, is the kind of tired that comes from not living the way you were designed to live, from quietly boxing with your own soul all day.

I feel sure we were made to make. The sad part of our specialization and globalization and _____ization is that we just don't have to make that much anymore. If our hands were moving more often to turn nothing into something, our hearts would slow down more often to meet the pace of our hands and we would feel less often like we're living in a fog.

The tricky part about this reality is that when we're tired, it feels like we just need to hurry up and sleep—that if we power through and work really hard, we'll finally be able to plop our feet up on some piece of cushy furniture and watch TV—or maybe just sit there and then go to bed early. Because that's what tired people do. They try to get more sleep.

Makes sense.

The problem, though, is that when it's our souls that are worn out, our hands that are quaky and itching to be used, shutting our eyes and lying still for nine hours isn't going to help us wake up rested. We'll feel less sleepy, but we won't feel any less rest-less, any less disoriented or off. I think we might need to think about tackling a different sort of rest for ourselves.

Please don't throw this book across a room because you are sleep deprived and mad at me for not understanding.

This is where I stop standing on top of my desk surrounded by weird stacks of fabric and jars full of old keys and boxes full of thread and I stop waxing on about living a life full of creativity, and I start talking about how mentally ill I felt when I couldn't get enough sleep. Because of All Those Kids.

It happens for stretches of time—like when our children are really small and unable to walk to the fridge for a glass of milk to get them through the night or when our jobs make us show up for week-long "retreats" that really ought to be called "Weeks Where You Will Have Meetings From Morning Till Night But We Will Feed You From a Trough In the Center of the Conference Table."

These times of life are real. They happen for short periods of time for many of us—and when I say "short" here, I mean "of a particular duration"—they are generally periods of time that have a beginning, middle, and an end. They might feel like we're living them in dog years, but one day we do wake up and realize that we got eight hours of sleep and that tomorrow night it could likely happen again.

So I don't want to skip the reality of living in a space that makes us really, physically exhausted. This is one kind of tired: Body Tired.

There's another kind, though, that is easy to mix up with Body Tired: it's Soul Tired. And sleeping doesn't help it. Sleeping doesn't touch it with a stick.

Soul Tired requires something different. And I think some of what it requires is more making. Generally, when I think about being Soul Tired, I think of living a life where

I'm doing lots of something I feel like I should do, and not enough of what I'm made to do.

Sometimes our souls want to hang out and enjoy themselves by making something. They want to lose themselves to time.

Your tired soul is in there ready to talk to you—and it would be smart of you to listen. Sleeping won't necessarily help you to hear what these things are. They are likely to be creative in nature: they are likely to be dancing or drawing or writing or set making or flower arranging. They are likely to be things that require you to look around and gather up scattered pieces of something and turn those scattered pieces into a whole something else. They are likely to be about making something.

Maybe you like to paint landscapes. Or old tables. Maybe you like to sew clothes for your pet iguana. Maybe you keep thinking about a stack of old t-shirts in the back of your drawer or your son's drawer or a stash of old baby clothes up on some garage shelf somewhere and how you want to make a quilt. Maybe you find yourself staring at old broken appliances and really wish you could make a lamp. Maybe you dream about welding.

The thing is, your soul is smart. It keeps waving its arms and pointing and stringing twinkly lights around whatever it is that it wants to do. It can't write you any notes and leave them on your car windshield. It can't require a single policy change of you, so it's left to repetitive suggestion. Whatever it is that your eye lands and stays on or wonders about, that's likely your soul trying to flag you down.

And maybe there is not a single thing that you can imagine like this. Maybe you have never wanted to make a single thing in your life.

Don't hit me, but I just don't buy it. I think it's more likely that your understanding of making is unnecessarily limited. You think in terms of the standard crafts or music or dancing. And you have never noticed that your garden is something you build colors with. You've never noticed that maps you've always collected and kept rolled up in your office closet are dying to be turned into something that could be stared at on your coffee table. And the wool blankets that you wash so carefully and stack and re-stack in your linen closet are calling out to you in their reds and blacks to tell you that weaving is something you could actually pull off.

It's okay if you don't have a single clue what to make. And it's okay if trying to figure it out makes your tired soul feel more tired. It doesn't mean you're not meant to try. You don't have to know why doing these things is going to help you. You don't even have to believe that making bird houses out of old license plates or carving soap will make you feel rested.

But what if they would?

SING IT OUT & GET IT DOWN
(WRITE)

Go for a walk and sing to yourself about how you spend your time. How do you spend it? What do you do? How did you end up spending your time the way you are now? What's the story of that evolution? And what do you wish you could make? If you don't like to write music, then pick a melody that you already know ("Camp Town Races" or "On Top of Old Smokey" are good songs for this) and start describing in song the thing you would do if you had all the time and all the money and all the people in your life wore little cheerleading outfits with the first letter of your name sewn onto the front while they watched you do it. What would you make? How would you spend your time? Sing about it. Then get down what you sang about. Grab a pen when you get back from your super weird singing walk and scribble about it. Otherwise, you might not remember all that great truth that popped in your head.

Make a quick list of all the people who stared at you and/or ran away while you walked around your neighborhood singing your head off about your deepest desires. You want to remember these moments, people. Yes: you may sketch them. If you're inclined, a full-blown watercolor might make you really happy later if you did it.

TIME SWAP

(go do this)

I can't prove it, but I think we actually gain some rest when we carve out space for ourselves to make things. So eight hours of sleep is actually less rest than six hours of sleep + two hours of making. I can't prove this math, but I Hereby Assert That It Is True. Try an experiment: choose three nights a week for a couple of weeks, and swap out one hour of sleep for an hour of sitting quietly and making something. Keep some notes. Did you wake up as sleepy? It's possible you will: this is an experiment. You might try a couple of different activities in a couple of different places. When the two weeks are over, really try hard to notice the difference that could be percolating in your insides. (You might need to talk to a friend before you start this to tell her what you're up to, and then talk to her again at the end so that you can have some help checking in about the impact of what you're trying.) Was there any activity in particular that added to your rest?

IF ALL THAT JUST MADE YOU MORE TIRED,
THEN CUT THIS PAGE OUT ON THAT
DOTTED LINE AND BURN IT WITH A TINY
MATCH. NO HARD FEELINGS.

I'VE GOT TOO MANY
UNFINISHED PROJECTS

I talked with a mom's group not long ago about the worth of maintaining your Creative Life while you're up to your neck in your Mom Life. They all nodded, but I could tell they thought I was batty. They all had that You have no idea look in their eye. And then I asked them to share about the state of their creative lives. And this one woman said, "I have so many unfinished projects." But she said it like she was saying, "I have so many moles on my A," or "I have so many unplucked whiskers on my chin." You know—with some sort of Lady Shame.

And it led into this discussion (well, that's not true because it was just me jumping up and down and talking excitedly) about how a creative life worth having isn't measured by final products. The goal of a life making things isn't supposed to be about *what we make*—it's supposed to be about *making something*. And a life spent making is a good life: it's a life where we learn about how screwing things up is inevitable. And that seeing pieces and turning them into whole things is incredibly gratifying. And that any life that includes doing something that we lose time to is a good life. And that when our souls slow down and stop hovering above ourselves to analyze our worth (or the size of our butts), that's time well spent.

Some of them got what I was talking about. Some of the others looked at me like they thought I was a really friendly nut job.

One of them asked me, "Do you finish any of them?"

And then I told her that sometimes I don't, but that I usually have upwards of 10 projects in play at a time. I do finish them, but not all of them. What I never do is wait to finish one thing before starting the next.

Then she looked at me like she wondered if I let the dishes stay in my sink for three or four days at a time too.

It's easy to believe that in order to allow ourselves to go forward, we need to finish what we haven't. This seems the most true, I notice, for people whose projects have been sitting for a long time.

Often, stuck projects are stuck for a really good reason, though. We may believe that we're the problem, but really the problem is with the project itself.

One of the reasons that I have unfinished projects is that I am likely trying to turn the project into something that it doesn't want to be. Sometimes projects just don't want to be what I want them to be. And when this happens, I am generally stubborn.

When the western shirt that I tried to remake out of pink cotton and an awkwardly-cute, pink skunk print did not come together as I'd imagined it would, I set it aside. I think I even put it in a baggie and marked it with a sharpie—shoved it in a closet. When I did this, I believed that the difficulty with the project was just that I am not good at following patterns. The work got tedious, and I got agitated. I figured I'd set it aside until I was better at making shirts.

When I pulled the thing out of the baggie a year later {*cough* Idon'talwayscleanoutmyclosetsthatoften *cough*}, the pink skunk shirt and I were at exactly the same stand off we'd been at when I shoved it in the bag.

This wasn't because I'm no good at sewing with a pattern, though. I'm sure of it now.

What I really think is that two hours into staring at that skunk fabric—which I'd hoped to be somehow ironic in its use for the western shirt—I realized I didn't like it. It would've been perfect for dental scrubs. But not on a shirt that I'd actually end up wearing.

Some part of me knew it would stay in my closet. And so a couple of the feet I use for making things just started dragging themselves. My insides had a tiny revolt that I didn't pay attention to.

The agitation wasn't from the tedious nature of the work: it was from my annoyance that I didn't actually like the fabric I'd chosen. But rather than listen to it talking to me (*You're just not ever going to wear me*, it kept saying), I told myself I was no good at working with patterns.

Sometimes this is the case: our unfinished projects are often unfinished for a really good reason that we just really don't want to hear because we've spent so much time on them already.

I've found that it's much more likely that I will take the time to finish a project that actually wants to be what I want it to be. Said another way, if I'd let the shirt turn into a ditty bag—which it would have been a really great combo of colors and textures and weird patterns for—then I probably would have been willing to learn the difficult-for-me-to-follow instructions for making the bag.

The difficulty wasn't that I couldn't make a shirt. The difficulty was that the shirt I was making didn't want to be a shirt, and I lost steam trying to force it into being something it didn't want to be.

There's another reason too, I think, that we have unfinished projects...

All projects require varying levels of heady inspiration and sweaty doing. Some of the doing is really tedious, and some of the imagining is really complicated. It's likely that we all favor one end of that continuum—the imagining or the actual making. And so sometimes we hit a spot in a project whose challenge doesn't match our current ability.

In that case we have to learn to do something we're not confident doing yet—or it might mean we need to try-and-rip and try-and-rip.

If we don't go in expecting to have to do this, we might get tripped up and just wait to somehow become better at it later. If we're working on a project that means a lot to us (like a quilt made out of our grandpa's shirts, maybe), we're less likely to relax into this sort of keep-trying-at-it way of proceeding. We're more likely to set it aside and wait to feel less nervous trying it.

You see the trap here, right? We wait to get better at something rather than working to get better by actually trying it. And then we never get any better and our waiting just turns out to be waiting.

Waiting just doesn't work. In fact, I'd say it makes it worse: we connect our creative lives to a project that gives us nothing but nauseous dread.

There's always a good reason a project is unfinished. Better to get honest about the reason and either backtrack the project to a spot where you do want to go forward or let it turn itself into something it actually wants to be. Don't wait for stuck projects to magically resolve themselves. I think you might be wasting a lot of time you could be spending making something.

Don't waste that time.

THE UNFINISHED OBJECT
THERAPIST (WRITE)

Take dictation for your stuck project. Pretend it's a shy person who doesn't like to speak up. Sit the project on a chair. Or lay it down on a couch. You sit in another chair. Be your Unfinished Object's therapist. Ask it some questions. Take out a paper and pen and —a steno pad if you can get your hands on one. *What do you always wish you were? What were your early aspirations? What did you wish you were going to be?* Write down what you hear. What is bothering the project about itself?

Listen to what it has to say. It knows what it wants to be and doesn't want to be. *Who were your early influences? What's going on with you these days? How do you feel being in the back of the closet? What do you wish you could be? If I just let you be what you want to be, how would you inhabit the world?* Let the project have a say.

What did your unfinished object say? It doesn't count as a breech of confidence to share it here because you are not an actual   therapist. And, um, if you are, your unfinished object is not your actual client—just to be clear.

GUTSY REDO (go do this)

Go to the closet where you keep the projects you haven't finished. They're stacked there for a reason. They are likely projects that started to turn in a direction that doesn't match your love of color or your skill level or your relationship with the person you're making it for. Sit down with the unfinished object. Stare at it. Look for the parts of it that you do like and the parts of it that you don't. Let it decide that it doesn't want to be the thing that you were telling it to be. Let yourself turn it into something completely different. Maybe that quilt wants to be a big pillow cover backed in butter yellow. Or maybe the one sleeve of the sweater you're knitting for your kid's teacher wants to be a plastic bag holder. Stop waiting to get motivated to finish something that you've not wanted to finish for months or years. Start listening to the project. Let yourself have the guts to do something different with the project than what you initially intended.

(Tell the truth: what did you want it
to be?)

(What did you end up letting yourself turn it into?)

IT IS TOTALLY OKAY IF YOUR UNFINISHED
OBJECTS JUST SAT ON THE COUCH AND
STARED AT YOU. DON'T FEEL BAD OR
ANYTHING. THEY'LL SPEAK UP ONE OF
THESE DAYS IF YOU JUST KEEP LISTEN-
ING ...

I CAN'T MAKE ANY MONEY AT IT

It seems like if you own a hot glue gun then somebody tells you to open an etsy shop. No judgment: I've done it. And I know lots of wildly gifted, patient, steady-working makers who do. I'm glad to be able to purchase what they make.

But not all of us were cut out to sell the goods we make. I tried to put a really cool purse that I made out of a vintage placemat covered in clowns up there. I tried to find the right price to sell it. $3,000? Oh, ok $49. I tried to wait long enough for people to look at it and take the Visa leap to actually buy it.

But I yanked it down after is sat there about nine days without selling. I couldn't swing the tension of it all.

There's a sort of strange mental looping that my brain does around selling what I make that has made me wonder if selling handmade goods is such a good idea after all.

Here's how the torture goes:

Me to Myself: If I like sewing so much then shouldn't I do it as a job?

Myself to Me: Sure, what a good idea.

Me: Well, if I'm going to do it as a job, how much would I need to charge? How much would I need to make?

[she scribbles numbers down, writes in a book, and then stop and stares]

Myself: Oh. Well, that won't work.

Me: So if I love this so much but I can't do it as a job, shouldn't what I make at least be so wildly popular (as rated by others) that people sweep in and pay large amounts of money for it? Sub question: How much would I need to see people paying in order to BELIEVE that it was Wildly Popular?

Myself: Oh. Well, that's not happening.

Me: So if that's not happening, then this must be a Wildly Un-Popular Undertaking.

Myself: So why am I doing it?

Me: And (here comes the downward spiral) why is it so lame anyways? And should I maybe be embarrassed of it? Who would even pay for what I do anyways? [slump.]

Myself: I'll just give it all away as gifts.

And right there is the moment that every single gift I give becomes a weird, inwardly apologetic moment of consolation to me, devoid of joy, a Jr. Varsity Happening. This sort of dialogue can occur for me over a period of months or within a single day, and is inevitably re-set by some sort of Pep Talk + Carbs. And then I step out into another day, at any moment vulnerable to fall headlong into the same Pit of Crafting Despair.

I have come to the conclusion, friends, that it's not so much money I'm always wanting, as it is the message that receiving money would give me: *You are good enough and smart enough and people like you enough.* Sort of a Stuart Smalley Self-Talking-To that would justify my hours upstairs surrounded by old polyester while my kids run around downstairs with knives eating nothing but boxed food and my husband languishes in a corner watching old Office episodes.

Somehow, in my mind, Money = The Internal Justification for Time to Sew (insert the name of whatever undertaking you absolutely love but make no money doing).

And that, I have come to realize is very, very tricky math. What happens, for instance, if the people around you are just like you and don't have or plan to spend a lot of money on anything they love to do? What happens if your personal aesthetic {*cough*} is unusual {*cough*} and not every single person {*cough*} shares it?

And so, at least for now, I have unplugged myself from that metaphor. The electric socket that it's running through is marked Capitalism (Roughly: my supply not bumping up against a Demand = my non-viability.) And I'm hereby plugging myself into a different metaphor. This one includes bunnies and unicorns and people dressed in weird costumes jumping around a lot--something to do with the circus, maybe.

Am I slamming others who sell their stuff? *Holy Toledo, No.* Am I saying I'll never have a shop EVER? *Holy Toledo, No.* Am I a Socialist or something? *Well, Holy Toledo, Sometimes.* So do I wish I could sew all the time and do nothing else but write about it? *Holy Toledo, Yes.*

Some of what I wonder about all of this selling what we make is whether the stuff we make is actually what we're selling. In fact, are we selling anything at all? —or are we trying to buy something?

I think sometimes we pop open etsy stores because we want to know if anybody besides our best friend or our favorite grocery store clerk thinks the stuff we make is any good. We want validation from strangers. We want to know if we're really a maker. Are we allowed to say that this thing we do with old wood and moss and the laces of our children's baby shoes is something more than a hobby?

And so we think that maybe if we pop it up into internet space and some people who don't go to our church actually spit out 15 bucks for it, then, well, maybe we're good at it. Maybe we're meant to be a maker.

Maybe we shouldn't be entrusting our souls to strangers in this way. Right? And maybe, just maybe, if we are good with the wood and moss and the baby shoe laces, but not so good at the marketing or the pricing or all that Make an Internet Button And Then Get Your Friends Who Blog To Put It Up On Their Site So You Sell More. Well, then, maybe our beautiful pieces are never found.

And maybe then we have accidentally sold more than our lovely artwork. We've put up some other thing for sale—some thing that has to do with the chance to tell ourselves that a life spent making things is a good life. And that we are allowed to live a life like that.

That's not what etsy was made to sell. I don't want us to sell any of those things. I want us to hold tightly to those things. To treasure them. To make little blankets for them to sit on out on a porch somewhere when it's hot. To bring them iced tea and crackers on plates. To welcome them as extra people in our houses.

If your store is making your soul hurt, take it down, friend. If it's making your insides strain, and you find yourself clicking your admin site to see whether anybody new has favorited the gorgeous vintage sheet dress you just put up, then I want to encourage you to consider taking a little vacation.

I wanted to type, "...to consider shutting down shop." But this seems extreme, and we've never met. I do, though, want you to consider just pushing the pause button. You might be accidentally handing over some part of your insides that you ought to hold on to. Are you selling only what you're making? Or are you trying to buy the right to make things?

Just a couple of questions to keep you up at night.

In the meantime, hear this: you were made to be a maker. What you're making is lovely. I'm sure of it. The way that you take time with the part that you know is important to stop and really take time with, it's important. The way you think about the person you're making for. The way you like to mix the color and imagine the thing in the home of the person who will have it later, this is all really good stuff. And you ought to keep doing it.

You know the parts of the process that really buoy you— that make you feel a little lighter inside, and your heart believes that some part of that buoyancy is transferred to the one who picks up the thing you made. And you're right. It is transferred. And you ought to keep doing all that handing over of lightness. It's a great kindness to the world when you do it.

And also, if you do feel like it's time to take down your store for a bit, it's okay: there's going to be a time when it might make a whole lot of sense to put the shop back up again. I think once our insides get settled around these things, then a store can be a lovely thing to have. Great, actually. If we can manage to have a financially viable making life, then that's the one that we want to have. If we can sell four handmade burp rags a month and pull in 60 bucks and that floats our glue and driftwood habit, then we oughtta do that.

We just don't want our stores to be anything else than that, though. We don't want our maker's hearts muddied in the mix of all those dollars. Our souls are just too precious to be priced like that—even if we ever do figure out a way to hit a profit that outruns time and materials.

(WRITE)

WAY FANCIER MATH

You likely already know if you're making any money selling what you make. Just a plain old income minus expenses sort of math problem will give you that number. How about doing a way fancier sort of math? Do you know what other currencies are important to you? Do you value sleep? Excitement? Access to chocolate? Time in the sunshine? Proximity to puppies? What are the things that make you glad? Are there any costs that are particularly precious to you? Are loud spaces taxing? Does the sound of other people sneezing really get on your nerves? Do you hate talking to strangers? What sorts of regular looking difficulties feel like they hit you particularly hard? These things are your currencies—they're the things to do a fancier sort of math about for yourself. First make a list of Glads and a list of Super Bads. Then see if the selling of your handmade goods intersects with these. It could be that your store is pinging right off the Glads list. Or it might be that you are enduring a long list of hidden Super Bads. I'm not saying I know: I'm saying I want you to know.

(go do this)

GLUING POTLUCK

Sometimes it's great to gather together other people who are just as crazy about making as you are. Host a Gluing Potluck. Don't feel pressured to cook something fancy and have all of your attention on whether or not your butterflied quail arrives to the table hot enough. Have a potluck. How about a salad bar potluck? Just make sure that you melt a pound of cheese on top of a loaf of bread so that no one starves. Tell everybody to bring old magazines. Put somebody else—not you because you're having the thing at your house and you'll need to have time to dust the toilets—in charge of bringing the poster board. If your friends have big personalities, you'll need big poster board. If you roll with quieter people, cut these into smaller boards so that they won't overwhelm. Put lots of scissors and glue and old magazines or sale ads in the middle of the table—or even better in the middle of the floor—and start cutting and gluing. There's no theme. Just cut what you feel like cutting and glue it where you feel like gluing it. Make something together that you'd never try to sell.

(Your Gluing Potluck Guest List)

PRETEND YOU WALK IN THE DOOR AND ALL OF THOSE PEOPLE ARE ALREADY SITTING ON THE FLOOR GLUING STUFF. WHO IS DOING WHAT? AND HOW HAPPY ARE YOU TO PLOP DOWN IN THE MIDDLE OF THEM ALL AND JOIN IN? I KNOW. THAT'S MY WHOLE POINT.

I DON'T HAVE ANY ROOM

C laiming a creative space has always been a challenge
for me. I haven't always been sewing, but I have
always been writing—and I've always had the
feeling that I needed a Writing Spot. I once cleaned up the
shed that held my apartment complex's washer and dryer
and set up a table and chair between the two machines so I
could write the poems I was churning out at the time.

Another time I put a table in my living room. Once I
had a desk in an abandoned garden shed. And once I put
one in the weird TV/Romper Room we had when the boys

were little. (I was writing at the desk; they were writing on the walls.) I have always had a writing desk. Everywhere I've lived I've made space for it.

And here's what I've found: I've never written much at it. I never wrote in the laundry room. I wrote in that garden shed only because I was writing for cash at the time. (I didn't write any poems back there.) I could fit my son's bouncy chair on the floor next to me and wobble it with one foot while I typed. It was the place where I set up the printer. Where I kept all the pens and paper. But when I wanted to write—really write—I usually did this on a strange scrap of paper while I was vacuuming the living room. Or other times in a coffee shop. Or flying on an airplane.

I've needed the desk. And I've also never needed it a bit.

I think what I've really needed is some sort of physical declaration that I am a writer. A stack of furniture and gear that elbows the people around me out of thinking that I'm not a writer. A physical proclamation of my identity.

And now I have a room for making things. It's upstairs, off from the rest of the house. And it's true that I go up there sometimes, but mostly it serves as a sort of monstrous closet for the stuff that I make with—like the messiest closet you've seen in your life, actually. It really could just as easily be set up in a big corner of my garage.

Don't get me wrong. I love the space. But I notice that I can make just about anywhere. Lately I'm crocheting big rugs out of old sheets. I do this on the living room floor or on the couch in front of the TV while everybody walks around just really thankful that my project doesn't include needles that they could step on. At one time I made nothing but aprons. I made these at the dining room table, and I would scooch all the fabric down to the end of the table when it was time to eat. Classy.

It's true that we need physical space to be makers. And a room is a fantastic gift. But I think that when we make a different kind of room inside ourselves—the kind that settles it for any questioning part of our heads that we are, in fact, meant to be makers in the world, then the room is just that. It's a spot for dumping fabric and leaving sewing machine thread all over the floor.

If we don't need it to tell ourselves or anybody else that we're meant to be making what we're making, then it probably can be less fancy than the dream studio we're all waiting to have some day, which is what I hear from people about their creative lives: they'll get to it some day when they've got more space. When they've got the room.

To which I always want to say (but never do quite pull out the guts to say to their faces—mostly because we're usually at somebody else's wedding standing at the cheese table, and I try not to ask deep, existential questions in settings like these for fear that I will accidentally undo someone): "Um. Why don't you have the room?"

So I guess I'll just ask you, "Why don't you have the room?"

I don't mean a designated room in your house. Lots of people don't have that. But why don't you have space for the things you love to make with? You've made space in your house for food, for everybody's clothes and gobs of shoes and your roommate's five bikes, for weird stacks of photos, for everything your mother-in-law left behind when she died, for soccer cleats that don't fit anybody you even know anymore, for 14 years worth of tax returns, three surf boards, five scooters, boxes of paper goods for when you give parties, your godmother's china, nine musical instruments. Why don't you have the space for the making that you like to do?

Why haven't you made a space? Even a little space? A beautifully organized bucket located in an easy-to-get-at spot. The bottom of a coat closet. Or the top of a coat closet. Or one half of your linen closet. Or a drawer. Or three buckets in your garage. Or an armoire in the corner of your living room. Or a table in the family room. Or a chest in your bedroom. Or a shelf somewhere. Or 30% of your garage? Why don't you have the space?

Maybe a better question to ask is this one: "Why do you have the space for all that other stuff?"

When your pantry is overcrowded, you go to the hardware store and buy all kinds of white plastic stacking thingies to make the space useable. When your daughter wants to do more art, you buy her a sweet little desk and those cute little buckets for her scissors. When the garage is bulging with bikes, you engineer a solution to keep people from breaking their legs in there. You have the ability to address the needs of your household. Why haven't your need for some space to make stuff?

It could be that you think of it as "unnecessary"— somehow it's "extra"—like making room for a pinball machine for the garage. Or a soda maker. Or a swinging chair in the backyard.

What if you decided that it was important for you? Then

I bet you could do something really nifty with a corner or a closet or an attractive stack of buckets. I just bet you could.

I suspect that you could find a way to make room for yourself in your house if you decided that it was important enough.

A room with a door that closes totally helps. I'm not going to lie about this. But I don't want you to wait to start making until you can have this. Because that might mean waiting until somebody moves out or you can afford a bigger house. And maybe you need to jump into your making life before one of those things happens.

Maybe it would help if you began to see "storage space" and "work space" as separate functions of a studio. Most of what I hear from people when they don't have a dedicated room is that they don't want to "make the mess." I get this. Nobody likes to fall into a reverie of hot glue and pigeon feathers only to have to do all that sweeping later so everyone else can eat dinner...but maybe there is another way. Could there be a corner of your garage where you built a sort of drop-down desk space? Is there room in your laundry room for a table? Do you have some lovely antique roll top desk that's currently holding your bills that would better hold your making supplies—so that when you had a little time to grab, you could pop the thing open and then just close it all up and hide it away when it was time to switch gears?

Could it be that you're waiting to tell yourself that one of the things you really are is a person who likes to make things? Maybe if you went ahead and told yourself that, then you'd believe yourself when you also said: Makers need room to work. Where will I set up?

FAKE ARCHITECT (draw)

Go draw a blueprint. You're not an architect: you're a fake architect, so just draw the rooms in your house as best you can. Label the Doing Zones. What do you do in those rooms? What are their main functions? Now label the Stuff Zones. What stuff are they filled up with? Where's are the hutches and stacked buckets and armoires? What are they full of? If you like math, calculate the percentage of square footage you're giving to the sorts of things you're handing your space over to. If you like pictures and not numbers, think about color coding the areas. The goal here is to give yourself a quick visual of what space is being given to what sorts of stuff. Does it add up for you? Are there any zones in your house that are going unused? Any activities that are taking up multiple zones? Any hutches full of things like paper goods or the china that you use only when your in-laws visit that could be moved into nice soft, padded buckets somewhere near where your washing machine lives?

Then draw a second blueprint: what would you like the zones to be used for? Where could you make the space for your making life? Look for it. Draw big arrows that point to it. Stare it at for a little while. Start to imagine how it could really happen. You could make room for your making life.

(Copy of the blueprint taped here for safe keeping…)

HUNTING FOR 3'S (go do this)

Now that you have a sense of your space, start in with the heavy lifting. Begin to look at the things taking up the corners and shelves of your house in terms of the immediacy of your need to have access to them.

> 1 = *You need to get to it daily*
>
> 2 = *You need to get to it weekly/ monthly*
>
> 3 = *You need to get to it once in a while*

Go hunting for your "3's." If right now you've got stuff that you need every-once-in-a-while access to and it's taking up easy-to-access space in your house, maybe it's time to reconsider where it's living. Do the special mementos left by your sweet mother-in-law need to be on a shelf at arm's reach in your laundry room? Do your children's artwork or a box of letterhead from the business you closed last year need to be in your desk drawer? If you can begin to look at your stuff in terms of how quickly you need to get to it, you might find some space you could begin to use for your making life.

There's nothing wrong, after all, with using your attic or the top shelves of the unit in your garage for something that needs a ladder. You're not getting rid of the stuff entirely (not, of course, unless you realize that it's time to)—you're just making smart use of the space you've got. Once you've hunted for your threes, start putting them on higher shelves to make some room for yourself on the ones you can reach.

MAKE YOUR LIST RIGHT HERE OF THREES AND
WHERE YOU STASHED THEM (JUST IN CASE YOU
REMEMBER IN A MONTH THAT YOU DID THIS
EXERCISE BUT YOU DO NOT HAVE THE FOGGIEST
IDEA WHERE YOU STASHED THE STUFF YOU DON'T
GET TO REGULARLY.) I KNOW: YOU ARE WELCOME.

I CAN'T BALANCE IT

There we are at the dinner table with dinner ready—not even cold yet—everybody's milk still unspilled, the kids bathed and ready to talk about the day's "thorns and roses" and even though I know that this is the sweet stuff of life, I'm running mental laps around the possibilities of a quilt that wants to be made for my brother's baby. And which vintage sheet would be best for the binding. And whether or not I should stamp something sweet on white sheets and add that to the mix too.

I'm at the table, but I'm really somewhere else.

On good days, this can look like mild distraction, on bad, overly-tired days it can look like all-out grumpiness.

And then you can only imagine what happens when the milk does ultimately spill…onto the pot roast.

But I'm stuck: if I get up and leave my family in a full-brown flee from the table, I feel bad. But if I stay and eat with them, I feel bad then too. My desire to make something can put me in a state where I start to feel bad no matter what I do—whether I stay or go, I feel crummy. How am I supposed to do all of it?

I know it's tempting to want to avoid this tension. I've heard lots of people say that they don't want to feel pulled, so they just don't try to make the time.

But that's no good, right?

The truth is that we don't always need as much time as we think we do. *I just need to leave for a week and do nothing but paint.* No you don't. I mean—sure, you do: but you can't just stop your life and step off of it all of the time.

The thing to do is to get good at telling yourself the truth about what might help. When I'm honest with myself about what I really need, there's a better chance I'm going to get it. And it's not always as dramatic as I'd imagined.

Some nights I really should just politely excuse myself and risk the potential frustration of my family and head upstairs. I need to have some scissors in my hand and for everything to be quiet-ish around me. I need some space to make something. Some nights it's just the best thing for all of us. Who needs a grouch at the dinner table?

Other nights, though, if I'm honest about what I need, it might not be all that intense alone time. It could be that I could grab a pile of sheets to rip up and crochet and plop in front of whatever strange family show we're currently addicted to and sit in the midst of it all and have some fun of my own at the same time.

There's a chance that I could get exactly what I need without having to drop everything and disappear. I just need to be really good at knowing what sort of making I'm hankering for.

It's helped me to be know generally which part of a project I can enjoy with other people around and which I can't.

The early part of my own creative process on any given project looks like me sitting on the floor surrounded by 25 clumps of fabric that I've grabbed off the shelves because they were talking to me that day. I stack them on top of one, listening to see which piece of fabric wants to talk to another. It's Project Fishing. I'm waiting to see if one piece of old polyester wants to make friends with some other piece and then waiting to hear if either of them are interested in being filled with books or maybe just something smaller and less weighty like an iPod. Or if they rather be made into a picnic quilt. I sit surrounded in the quiet. My job in that part of the process is to wait and listen.

And then I often sketch it on a page of my idea journal. Or I skip this part and just start cutting it up, and I begin to build.

This sweet, quiet receptivity rarely happens for me when I'm attending to other things. I don't do it easily while making dinner or watching TV. I can't help anybody with homework (at least not very kindly) while engaging in it. I really need to be alone to enjoy it. I've never done this in a crowd—at least not a crowd I was paying any attention to.

The next part of a project is the fun part for me: the building. And if I'm still making my way, if I'm trying to figure out whether or not my idea is actually going to work, I usually need to be on my own. This is often the stage of the process where I feel less calm and more anxious to see what will happen with a piece of turquoise and white polka-dotted polyester. I'm excited. I want the thing to start to be, and so if I have to leave or attend to something else at the same time, I'm probably annoyed because I'm excited.

I think this stage of the creative process is the easiest one to believe falsely that we can do with others around. We tell ourselves things like, "I'm just going to sew up a few seams," but we don't mean it. What we want to do is go make something. The desire is real. This is the one that I've found to be the most frustrating to do while my family is around. (Even if I haul the sewing machine downstairs.)

And what about going ahead and just sitting in the middle of everybody and getting your creative time that way? Does it work?

Well, yes: sometimes.

I think we've just got to get clear about what sort of making can reasonably be done in the company of three seven-year-olds and a junior high boy. Or with friends over. Or over at a friend's house. Or in the middle of church. What kind of making can I do while also doing something else? What sort of project can I do and not feel interrupted if I need to put it down to help someone butter toast?

Never do the part of making that you need to do alone when there are other people around. You'll be crabby about it. You really will—even if you try not to be. Everything about you will scream "go away" even if your mouth says, "Sure, honey, you can use that piece of fabric." Know what you can do and what you can't with other people around. Then do both kinds of making when it makes the most sense.

I could give a list here of things that are possible to pull off with others around, but it would just be mine. (Okay: it's crocheting, hand-sewing, and quilt-binding. There: you know.) Your list might be very different.

It has also helped me to keep an idea journal so that when an idea does comes, I jot it or sketch it quickly while I can see it in my head. I can even do this while stirring soup or in the waiting room of the doctor's office or while talking to someone who is taking a bath with a big-chested doll and a plastic horse. This makes me feel as though I have a means to keep the creek of my maker's life running while I'm down in the house with the rest of everybody—and I get a lot less of that "dammed up" feeling.

There's the thing, too, of sometimes living in a house full of kids who also like to make things, and so I sometimes feel like I should include them. You might feel this way about your kids or your roommate or your really talented (knitting) cat. You should include others in your project sometimes. If you do, you're a generous, wonderful, life-giving person who is making the world a better place. I say go for it.

I also say: don't get it confused with your regular making

life. Helping another person on a project they're excited about is living out your teaching life, sourced by your gift of encouragement, your penchant for making sure somebody else never feels stupid when they want to try something new, your desire for another to find what you've found in making. This is good stuff worth walking toward.

It's just not the same thing as Making.

I'm not saying it won't give you a buzz; I'm just saying it will be different. And I want you to hear me say that it's not the same thing. Even if the end product of both chunks of time produce a nine-patch square in your hands, the experience of the hour produces two entirely different things in your heart: and actually, if you're trying to do them at the same time, they'll produce a third thing only: frustration.

Make space for both kinds of things.

So sure, on some Tuesday night you might pull out the big jar of buttons and fire up the glue gun and spread paper clips all over the dining room table and say, "Have at it kids—just don't burn yourself." And you might sit there with them and mindlessly glue things. But you won't. You'll let the 12 year old be in charge of the glue gun, he'll burn his finger, and his brother's finger, and within seven minutes, you'll find yourself walking around the edges of the table holding a glue gun and gluing everybody's buttons onto everybody's paper clips for them. Or you'll just be in charge of getting the bandaids.

And this actually has all the makings of a fantastic little handful of moments with your kids or small friends or talented animals—unless, of course, you had your heart set on just sitting there and letting your soul hum as you sort of rocked back and forth gluing buttons to paperclips.

Go ahead and do this with a big smile on your face some Tuesday night. And then on the following Tuesday, don't— on the following Tuesday, take the buttons and the paper clips off to some other room, or wait until nobody else is awake anymore when you scatter them all over the table. And do that kind of button gluing, the kind that's Making.

And then the Tuesday after that, let all those kids just watch a movie, while you sit with them to watch, pull out your big weird bag of scrap crochet and start single crocheting a laundry line for your camper. Only let them jump in if they have their own strips of fabric and their own crochet hook—and they know how to use it. If they don't know how to crochet, tell them, "Let's learn next Tuesday!

(WRITE) A TINY PIECE OF A PLAY

Write a dialogue. Not a whole play, People: just a dialogue
with some details. The characters are **Real You** and **Current You**. You're having a conversation about your Making

life. It starts like this:

```
[On the porch]

Real You: Hey, Current Me, How's your
Making life?

Current You: What do you think? It
sort of sucks.

Real You: Why? What's going on?

[Dog enters and licks Current You's
leg]

Current You: Well...
```

Now finish the conversation. If you don't want the dog to
enter, well then don't have the dog enter. Have somebody
else enter. And if you need to describe the outfit that Real
You and Current You are wearing, or their hairstyles or
their tones of voice, then surely go ahead and do it. Get
them talking truthfully to one another. Include the rest of
the cast. Where do they walk? Who interrupts them? Is it
raining or sunny? How do they respond? If they're shy, be
patient. When "Current You" says "I don't know"—just
wait. She'll come up with something if you give her a little
time to talk and keep yourself from telling her what to do.

FUZZ-TIPPED STICKS (go do this)

Build something with LetteroftheAlphabet sticks.
You know—those things you're not supposed to
stick in your ear? You'll need three or four boxes.
Make sure you've got lots. Build something—anything. Start making something with these little
pieces of stacking goodness. It doesn't matter
what it is. Just make something. It won't live on
very long beyond the moment of your making
it. Somebody will knock it over with a football
or a wine glass or their tail. But make it anyway.
First, do this with unruly people—either drunken
friends or little kids. Then do this again alone.
Go somewhere quiet. It doesn't have to be dark
out, just quiet. And if it's too quiet and you start
to feel sort of twitchy, then turn on your favorite
music—maybe the soundtrack from your favorite
movie ever. Later, do this a third time while you're
making dinner or pulling off some other house
task. Set it all out on some part of the counter
that's not covered in tomato sauce and try building
while you stir soup.

You already know how different these moments would be. Do them so that you can know specifically how different they really are for you. You might be crazily surprised, friend—both by what you love in each run at the making time and by what makes you edgy…And maybe by some other stuff you and I can't even guess at right now.

(Draw what you built—or if you're really tricky,
take a picture and tape it here. Ohhhhhhh. Fancy.)

IT'S JUST TOO HARD

Okay. So it all makes sense, but your insides are still just not having it. If they had a head to shake at you, they would. Sometimes life is just overwhelming and the resistance is deep. You see the stuff in your life keeping you from living the way you want to—and your heart still won't budge.

I really do get it. Sometimes we're so deeply tired it's hard to even lean forward a little—even when we want to, even when it makes perfect sense in our heads. It's still just too hard.

If you were here with me at my table, I'd want to know your story, I'd want to make us a cup of tea and I'd say, "Tell me about what's making you busy…" (after I waxed on and ranted uncomfortably for like 20 minutes about how old polyester is good for everything and why everybody should be making something.) I would take a breath. Or you would fidget or something. Or I'd see the clock and realize how long I'd been talking. And then I would take a little nervous breath and remember what I'm trying to remember: everybody's got a story. And I want to hear a lot of them.

And then I'd sort of sit still long enough for you to believe that I really do want to know. And then maybe you'd tell me. About your mother who's lost big pieces of her memory and how you are caring for her. About your job and the way your boss seems to want you to get two days worth of work done in one day. About the ways that you grouse at your kids more than you want to and how this doesn't make any sense because when you are at work all you want is to be with them. About the way you used to sew. Used to write. Used to glue things for fun on Saturdays. Before you had kids. Before your husband got sick. Before you got the job you're in right now.

And I would ask more questions, I think. I mean, I hope I would.

"Who taught you to sew?" "What kind of sick is he?" "How old are your kids?" "What's your favorite part of your job?" "How often do you feel like throwing things?" "What's your favorite color thread?"

And maybe after a little while you'd start to notice that

you were telling me all sorts of truth you haven't thought to tell yourself or your best friend yet. Or maybe you'd just get up and leave (because sometimes I really do ask questions that are way too personal)

But then maybe you'd hear your story too.

I used to love to make dresses for my daughter when she was a baby. Picking out the fabric out was my favorite part.

My grandmother taught me to sew. We would do it together in the summertime when my parents went on vacation and left me at her house. We made cakes those summers too.

I'm not sure what kind of sick my husband is. I just know that I'm really tired, and I don't know how I'll keep going if I don't change something about the way that all of my hours are spent caring for him and none of my hours are spent filling up my own soul.

My favorite color thread is orange. But I haven't bought any for years.

My kids look at me in the eye more when I'm calm. And they yell less, sometimes bring me little trays of things as delivered offerings.

My daughter sleeps with the quilt I made for her while I was pregnant. I remember sewing late at night, so tired, but too excited to go to sleep, thinking of her and how she would be with us soon, and how someday she'd sleep with the blanket I was making.

And then I'd probably—I mean, if it were a good day— try not to say too much else.

Because you would have said some things out loud that maybe your own soul has been waving its hands about at you for a while now.

And if some of what you said in a really sincere tone of voice to me was, "What if I really, really don't have the time (in addition to being in denial about the nervous avoidance that's sprung from my own un-checked perfectionism)?"

Then I would take a risk. I would tell you what I really think—first that I really do believe you. And that some weeks I feel like I'm on a bad carnival ride that nobody will let me off of. But if I felt sure that you really wanted to know what I thought about the debacle of No Time, I would say this very quietly to you: "make the time."

It seems too simple, so don't throw the book across the room: I'm sorry. I don't have a pill or a time machine for this. Make time.

Do I think you should never spend any time with your kids and that when they cry and ask you not to go upstairs to sew again that you should cold-heartedly tell them, "No, mommy has boundaries now and she needs time for herself"? No.

I know that sometimes there's this 90-minute stretch in between when they do all go to bed that, if you were nice to your spouse-person about, he/she/they would probably high-five you for choosing to use the time to prop your insides a bit rather than scrolling through the menu of some online movie site looking for a movie that you will not have the time to watch. I think there's a chance that they will notice that you are, if a little sleepy in the morning, sort of in a better mood. (It's because you made something that you're in a better mood, if I haven't mentioned that.)

It's really possible that your schedule is too full for you to pull off the intricately patterned quilt that you've imagined making from your grandpa's shirts, the soft plaid ones you've kept in a box in the back of your closet since he died when you were in your twenties. It's possible that you're too busy to take a pottery class (even though you remember really liking it when you did it for a bit in college). It's really possible that when you wake up in the morning that your mending pile has overtaken your sewing basket and that the thought of making something actually makes you feel more stressed.

Deep, deep tired is rough. I really do get it. And I don't think that any of these projects make a lick of sense for you right now.

High stakes, complicated projects will make a soul-tired person more tired if she hasn't learned to relax into them. So start small. Crochet a washrag out of strips of jersey cotton you cut from an old t-shirt. Make one quilt square—just like a really easy one made out of the scraps of stained napkins you were about to give away. And don't do it with those precious flannel shirts. Do it with rags if you want. Or with some weird pair of pants that have never fit you but you paid full price for and can't get yourself to chuck from your closet.

Just trying making a little thing with a little time.

It will feed you. It will work to wake you up in a way that sleep won't. It will help.

WONKY CARTOGRAPHER (draw)

Draw a map of your best neighborhood as a kid. I
don't mean draw a picture of your house. Draw a
map. Remember the maps in front of those chapter
books we loved? Make one of the neighborhood
where you grew up. Draw it by hand. Make it
with pencil if you want so you can erase like crazy
to make yourself feel better if you're that way. Or
make it with pen. Get a stack of paper so that if
you mess up you've got extra right there. If you
want to make the map bigger, just tape another
piece of paper to the whole thing. Do you want to
do anything else to your map? Will you populate
it with people? The names you used to describe the
places? The important houses? What everything
smelled like, maybe? Where's the place on the map
where you remember making something and never
wondering whether you were talented enough to
make it? The place where you embraced wonk
wholeheartedly? Where did your soul feel at ease—
your Perfectly at Rest place?

Put some sort of really fancy circle around the spot or a pirate treasure "X." Draw arrows to that spot and glue glitter to it. Remember what it was like to have a spot like that. That's the place you want to be pushing to claim: that's your spot.

A HAPPY KIT *(go do this)*

Some craft projects come in kits. You'll likely find them for embroidery or bead making or paint-by-numbers. They're excellent. If the grown-up ones look intimidating, go hunting in the kid aisle of the craft store. You could needlepoint a unicorn or paint-by-number a horse and stable scene. Sky's the limit, People. Just walk up to the kit section and buy the first thing you lean toward. Go get one for yourself. You need to make something uncomplicated and fun. Follow some directions—slowly. It's good medicine for tired people. And it's okay if you don't even feel like keeping what you made. Just sit in those straightforward directions like you would in a hot tub: restfully, in no hurry, happy to soak. Here's the thing: you don't even have to keep it when you're done. So if it's a paint-on-black-velvet project, it doesn't have to match your couch and go straight to a frame in the living room. You can totally throw it away. Nothing bad will happen to you. Trust me on this.

(Take a pic of what you made with your kit and
tape it here. Good job.)

THE
PERFECTIONIST'S
ANTIDOTES

THE PERFECTIONIST'S ANTIDOTES

Not just anybody can practice being brave, get unstuck, step boldly out into their creative lives in these ways. I mean, well, actually anybody could. There's no law against it. It's America. And it surely doesn't require a specific kind of talent.

What is does require is a capacity to fail. And not everybody seems to be working on practicing that. It seems like a lot of people are actually pretty set on the success end of the continuum. They want it to show up in their every moment.

What I've noticed about creative projects is that the more I step toward the possibility of failure (the more I take a chance that my good idea is good even when I'm not completely sure), then the more really good ideas have taken shape into polyester bags and hankie-soft quilts and ottoman covers and things like that.

But, as we've said, the "possibility of failure" is not really what those of us who take medicine for being perfectionists run across a field to embrace.

But the more I am able to do the equivalent of writing the word PERFECTIONIST on a tiny scrap of paper and throwing it into a campfire in a bold metaphoric statement of "No way, man," the better shot I have at pushing forward, hiking off toward some other country besides the one that I'm currently stuck in.

It's no easy business. We've all become perfectionists for really good reasons, and doing something different will need some good ideas. Otherwise we'll just backslide into our old way of requiring that everything we make looks like it does in the glossy magazine of our screwed up brains.

So go ahead and ask me: "What do you do when you start failing and it makes you practically have a panic attack?"

Well, I call my therapist. Or eat a big bowl of pasta or something.

Once I've done that, I remember that I'm only making one thing. (And if I'm not—then I reign it all in and start only making one thing.) This way I don't have to compare the final product to anything else that exists in the world.

I get loose and start over. It's okay.

In order not to go into financial apoplectic shock, I make with fabric that doesn't cost $18/yard.

And sometimes I host a making party so that I can remember that I'm not alone in the world.

And all of this seems to work for me, even though I've already told you that I am so fear-bound in general that I've been collecting chicken figurines for years and only recently noticed that my house was full of the replicas of my own soul. CHICKENS, ya'll. Chickens.

Here are some other things that have helped me and would likely help you on your road to practicing, um, Not Perfectness. Think of them as ways to set yourself up to be really successful at lots of little failures. And while that sounds like a strange goal, it's just the one you'll need in order to proceed.

I AM ABOUT TO GIVE YOU SOME REALLY GOOD TIPS THAT HAVE WORKED FOR ME. AND I THINK THEY'RE GOING TO HELP YOU. THEY'RE NOT LAME, I SWEAR.

#1 Work with Low Stakes Goods

I sew with what I lovingly refer to as "Rescued Fabric." This is actually the only fabric I sew with. I see ladies in the fabric store, all doe-eyed and concentrating like they're using a 10-key. They've got armloads of matching fabrics. Color combos that anybody would look at and go, "Yeah. Those totally go together."

But something about all of it just doesn't let me step in. I'm a little upset by the florescent lighting—and mostly, I don't really love it when fabrics match, per se. I want them to talk to each other, be in a sort of color conversation.

And I can't ever get fabric to talk in a store. It just sort of sits there, staring at me.

And also it's expensive. I don't mean overpriced. I just mean that when you work with retail goods, you head into a project with a price tag on your efforts.

When you're using retail goods to make with (fabric; pre-made stamps; shiny, perfectly stacked home store wood), they're yelling YOU PAID FOR ME, SUCKER at you while you're trying to turn them into something. And so the receipt for their payment becomes a piece of your design consideration. "Well, I need to make something worth 23 dollars."

And that's just a drag.

"Rescued Fabric" means that I'm paying just pocketfuls of change for the goods I work with. It's fabric that was going to be forgotten about if I didn't save it: but I did. So not only is it cheap, but I have a strong sense of having saved one more thing from that weird landfill that must be in Nevada somewhere that holds all of our trash.

I find my goods at a thrift store or a garage sale or on some high shelf of my husband's aunt's barn...somewhere like that, somewhere that requires some digging around. And then I rescue it from its sad little hiding anonymity and bring it back out in the world to be purposable. Fabric is always sad when it's hiding. It likes to be out where the people are.

To top it off, now that my friends and family know that I love to work with these sorts of goods, I often get gifts of the stuff. I don't even have to ask for it. Somebody else finds it and drops it on my porch for me. Like Christmas, but without all the stressful baking.

But what about all that cheap stuff I can find at the retail store? Yes, there are bargains to be found. There's something really powerfully freeing about using supplies that were on their way to the trash heap, though—a sort of lightheartedness.

It's not that retail fabric is overpriced. I'm just saying that it's priced. And that price tag seems to follow me through a project.

Also, it's organized in a way that somebody else thinks it goes together. And the lighting is often reminiscent of my 7th grade Home Ec class. Plus the place is crawling with strangers. (Strangers make me nervous. I know. Ask me later.)

Worst of all, I can't ever figure out what to do with the fabric until I get it home. My inward buzz is gone when I'm in a store. Maybe it's that I'm working with scarcity. My soul is chanting *I only have ten bucks I only have ten bucks I only have ten bucks.* The enterprise becomes about staying inside a limit. And while that can sometimes be a fun sort of conquering game, it doesn't always fill my head with endless possibility. I'm just really thinking about the cash.

I get home from retail priced stores with goods that waft a sort of "You paid. Better be good." back at me while I'm trying hard to transform them into something that may or may not succeed. It doesn't work for me to sit in creative freedom with the vision of someone nearby in a corner smoking a cigarette with its legs crossed and mumbling "Huh. That's what you're going to do with what you bought?"

There's the thing, too, about buying goods that are pre-matched. I can't for the life of me find fabric I love when it's all squished next to other fabric of similar color so it can't scream its own singularitude. I love diving into a weird pile of taped-up bundles of fabric that are different weights and textures and colors and eras and hand picking the stuff that tells me I should take it home. Then my task is small (and fun). I'm treasure hunting. When I arrive at a high stakes places for goods-hunting, I'm not digging for treasure... I'm, well, spending it.

I have also found that it's hard for me shell out $8 or $12 or $82 bucks for fabric I'm not sure what I'm going to do with later. I generally feel like if I'm going to pay full price, I better know what it's going to be. Mostly, all I can feel is my wallet burning a hole in my pocket. I've got about as much creative juice flowing through my body in that cash register moment as the morning I took the SAT.

When I work with low stakes good, there's an incredible freedom. When I screw up and cut it wrong or botch the whole deal, I never, ever, ever have to say, THERE GOES 82 BUCKS. I might say, "Good one, Ginger. When will you learn to baste?" But I won't have a financial conniption over my project failure.

Best of all, I get to have all my good ideas in the safety of the spot where I love to make—surrounded by more low stakes goods and my sewing machine that always gives me good company. And under my own weird poorly-staged lighting. And in the quiet. And with nobody talking to me—unless I've invited them up. And I get to have my ideas at the pace I want to have them. I'm not paying for parking. I don't (generally) feel stupid for taking too long to decide. I'm not embarrassed that somebody else might see what I'm working with and think it's lame.

I'm relaxed. I'm home. I don't have so much to lose, so there's a much better chance I'll take some risks.

And that's the fast track to real creative growth: setting myself up to take risks. It's the way that I'll get the maker's rush I'm always craving ever since I gave up downhill skiing when I was 19. It's the way I'll make mistakes and so then learn from them.

And I'm talking here about fabric—but go re-read what I just said and insert the word "wood" or "old metal" or "used popsicle sticks" or whatever it is that you like to use to make something.

There are lots of low stakes goods to be found—you'll be surprised what you start to spot when you start to look. People pile things in front of their houses. Your favorite stores have strange bins of scraps in unsuspecting places. Your relatives might have already tried to do what you're trying to do—and they might have the tools you need in their garage. Some lady down the street might gladly trade two used sleeping bags for her entire set of wood embossing tools.

Think about the things you're drawn to. What's stacked up in corners of your garage or in your biggest closet?

Photos? Driftwood? Vintage screws? PVC pipe? You've been thinking of it as "useful" for a good reason, likely. It might give you hints about what sorts of materials you want to start making with.

Start piling it all up.

#2 Become a Treasure Hunter

When I'm not making something, or jotting down notes about what I want to make, I'm hunting for goods to make with. The gathering-up and hunting-for is a big part of the fun.

I like to think of my making life as following the eat-local movement. A lot of us are getting the picture that it makes more sense to eat apples out of a neighbor's backyard in October instead of $4 grapes trucked and boated from freaking Provence. (I made that grape-shipping stuff up about Provence.) So we've started to train our taste buds to want apples in the fall and melons in the summer and rutabaga in November. (I made up the stuff about the rutabaga too.)

I've done the same thing in my sewing life that I'm shooting to do in my eating life: I buy local. In season. When it shows up at the thrift store, dirt cheap, funky and ready to grab, I buy it. And when I say "in season" I just mean "in the bin" because this kind of fabric shopping usually means finding pink bunnies in December and reindeers and holly in June. When it's ready to pick, I pick it.

Not a bad activity, really—trolling thrift stores. It's fun to do with friends, doesn't cost a trash can full of money, is available to do year round and hones your skills of perception.

As it happens, I've come to a place where I have about as much fun trolling for goods as I do putting them together. And in this way it's extended what I think of as creative time.

There's a huge freedom in it: I don't have to know what I'm going to make with what I find. I don't have to spend a lot of money. I sort of skip through the aisles letting myself say yes to the way my heart says "Hey—Get That." And in a funny way, all the yes of this treasure hunting starts to tell my making self that it's not a batty part of me: it's a legit part of me that wants things and can have them even if the rest of me hasn't been presented with a six-part plan for what's going to happen when it all comes home.

Plus, then I have this wonderful stash of stuff ready to work from. Right up in my own space. So when the mood—or the 13 minutes of freedom, or the rainy day where my kids have for some reason had to take Benadryl—hits, I go to my stash of fabric and sit in the middle of it and start putting one glob of it next to another glob of it. Then sometimes I add one more. And if I'm feeling really fancy, I pull from my bucket of old trims too. Wonderful aprony things happen then. Or lately sometimes bag-ish things. And new combos of color and thought pop up that I feel FOR CERTAIN would never come to me in the store.

People who make things gather supplies as they go. (What kind of supplies? *Exactly. You tell me.*) Supplies are whatever make you stop and stare and wonder about them. They're the stuff you keep picking up along the road or the store aisle or the thrift shop bin. If you're a particular kind of magnet, they're your particular kind of metal. The stuff just keeps showing up. And you might find that you feel you're supposed to display it, but it's likely you're supposed to pile it up and stare at it and wait to hear what it wants to be turned into.

Stop somewhere on your way home this week—a thrift store, I mean, or the spot at the back of the hardware store where they stack the free wood. Or the junk yard. Or wherever that place is where you've been staring at low stakes goods to make with. Go grab that stuff. You need it.

OH, YOU KNOW, DON'T WAIT LIKE A WEEK. GO FIND SOME TREASURE REALLY SOON. LIKE RIGHT NOW WOULD BE GOOD.

#3 Set Up a Maker's Pantry

Give yourself a central space to collect these things. A clean corner for housing your hot glue gun next to your special oil paint butter knives next to your crochet yarn and all those used digital clocks that you're not sure yet what you're going to do with. Oh, and the bits of rope you found in your garage. And the glue your aunt gave you when she heard that you are making cat scratching posts out of used industrial carpet tubes and old burlap sacks.

Let yourself have a Maker's Pantry.

You need a space to house all your treasures if you're going to work with low stakes goods. You need room. You don't have to require *a room* in order to claim some room. I think it might be time for you to say it's okay that you like to make things and that it will take up some room in your living space to do it. Plus, if you're going to let yourself gather up low stakes goods to make with, you'll need a spot to see the way they want to go together.

Don't knock out a wall of your living room or anything, but do go looking for a reasonable corner or alcove to set a hutch or a bucket. There's many more ways to claim space than just to send your high schooler to college a year early.

Put up a card table in the back of the garage. Rethink how much stuff is in your linen closet (do you need four sets of sheets for every bed in your house?) Or set up a shelf in the laundry room. Or in your closet. Or in the shed where you keep all those boxes of yearbooks from high school and bridesmaid dresses from the 80's and rusted bicycles. You know—that shed.

I'd encourage you to claim a space that you could easily see. Closed buckets in a back bedroom speak of a maker's space that is set up for "some day." It's likely that if you can't see what you've got, it'll be trickier to see how to use it all. If you use shelves in your linen closet—well, then all you have to do is open up a door. Why not put your extra sheets in the buckets in your back bedroom?

Deciding not to hide what you make with might be your first step toward claiming space.

And then maybe some day you'll find yourself clearing

away a corner in the garage. Or turning your "guest room" (that's used four times a year) into a maker's pantry (that would speak to your heart four times a week...at least. Plus—what overnight guest has ever complained about staying in a room that you also use for something else? See? My point.)

A designated spot to corral all your goods will help you have the chance to see one thing next to another. And it'll likely also help you to believe you really are meant to make things as much as you want to.

Once you get rolling with all this collecting of low-cost, low-stakes bunch of supplies to make things with, you'll need to take good care of it. It's actually possible to have too big a stash of goods to make with.

I know this seems impossible—who wants to say no to a carmely tan plaid swatch of 1970's polyester when it shows up in her favorite thrift store? Surely not me. There is a crucial moment, though, in building a stash of supplies for yourself when just throwing another option on the pile won't help.

Sure: get the carmel plaid. Who would ever pass up carmel-colored plaid? Hello.

But when you take it home, don't just throw it on top of the pile. Sometimes you need to sift through what you've got and pass on to somebody else all of the stuff that you are just owning to own. Sometimes there are some bits of cotton—some koi fish print, maybe—and you want to like it. Somebody gave it to you: who wants to waste a bit of free fabric?

When you look at it, something's just not right. Your eye stops on it in a way that seems to drown out your ability to see everything else that's there. Let it go. Put it in a pile to give to somebody else to get their stash started, or your favorite seven-year-old who loves to cut stuff up, or your kid's preschool.

As you build your own maker's pantry, plan to go into it at least a couple of times a year looking for goods that have gone stale for you.

You'll be amazed at what taking out distracting goods will do to what you decide to leave there. They will look much shinier, much fuller of possibility, with nothing making your eyes Somehow by subtracting from your stash of goods, you will have added something.

And you'll have a real pretty pantry.

#4 Make Lots of
Low Stakes Projects

I t's easy to be drawn to a project with lots of meaning.

Many people tell me that they want to make a quilt with their children's baby clothes someday. Or from their grandpa's shirts.

And these are lovely ideas. They really are.

But they're not necessarily projects that lend themselves toward practicing at how to fail. The stakes are just too high. Now that grandpa is gone, and the kids are grown, those small stacks of fabric have moved from the category of scraps to the category of precious—something that can't be re-found once it's messed with.

I would never suggest skipping these kinds of projects altogether, but I would say that having one of those in play alongside many other lower stakes projects would be a good move.

I recently found myself making clothes from old sheets for my daughter's buxom plastic doll. It was a lovely thing to do. After all, the doll's mouth is hermetically sealed shut. She couldn't complain a bit. And while my five year old did complain about the way that the shirt made the doll look pregnant because it shot up in the front, she never once said a thing about the bumpy hemlines or oddly-chosen fabric combos. There were no voices of doom in my head about the ways in which the apron (cut from the elastic edge of a fitted sheet so the little straps would stretch around her tiny, unrealistic waist) didn't seem as good as the ones in the box.

There was just lots of cutting and hand sewing and trying on and re-making. Lots of happiness, actually.

When your making life is filled with a combination of these low stakes projects (the more the better) and also include the higher stakes stuff (those things made out of really important bits of fabric or made for once-in-a-lifetime moments), then your maker self will be generally in a better state as well. I'm not saying don't make pretty stuff for important occasions: I'm saying pay attention to your ratios. If most of your projects are made for no good reason at all and also with goods that were about to be thrown out anyway, you'll find you'll enjoy yourself quite a bit more.

I almost always have at least four or five projects going at once.

Right now I'm finishing crocheting a pink scrap rug for my five-year-old; I'm quilting my trailer quilt (tentatively titled, "Tic Tac Toe In Church"); I'm piecing a quilt for my new niece; I'm *ahem* starting over on my street-sized living room rag rug, which I completely unraveled and put back together without that annoying pinkish sheet that ended up in there somehow. And I'm hoarding strange pieces of cardboard for some set of projects that I haven't quite yet put my finger on.

Those are the things in active play. They don't include the other weird Idea Piles that I have going upstairs. Because Idea Piles are something different than Works in Progress. Idea Piles are sort of testing grounds—like if I have an idea for what to do with a weird stack of fabric, then I pile it, and if I come back to it and I REMEMBER that it's an Idea Pile and not just a Stack of Fabric to Be Put Away That Somebody Must Have Left Right There In My Way, then it turns into a project. That's how that works. It's a sort of way to use my waning memory to temper my creative bursts.

And some of how I have the freedom to have so many projects in play at once is that it doesn't cost me much to have all the supplies for lots of projects, so there's almost always something I "feel" like working on.

There's also lots of piles.

So, go make a lovely little something. Something that reminds you that making a little means you're a maker. You get to pick what to make. Here are some possibilities:

* An off-season, non-yuletide popcorn string

* A long, single-knot crocheted laundry line

* Any kind of fabric, paper, or cardboard and ribbon bunting

Do one of these things. Just make one something.

#5 Stop Hoarding Failures

I used to open one of my supply closets and regularly have a full stack of flopped projects fall on my head. Embarrassing. First there was the part about being attacked by old polyester, and worse was the reality that they were all things I was bummed didn't turn out like I'd thought they would.

Not anymore. I say: give away failed attempts. Unless I plan to remake them, I send my botched jobs downstream to the donation center.

You might be hesitant to do this. But it's worked to clear the decks for me.

Are you kidding?! I worked really hard on that.

I believe you. But it didn't turn out the way that you wanted it to. I really am sorry about that, but I'm feeling like because it smells like failure that you might want to throw it out or hand it off. It's sort of stinking the place up.

Give me a break! I paid $72 for that yarn from sheep who watched cable and ate bon-bons and had therapy for their shearing memories.

I know it's hard to think about losing the money. Could the thing be taken apart and remade? It keeps telling you that you screwed up—and I think mulling over that failure every time you come across it in the closet is really very expensive for you. I'm sure there's an easier way for you to save $72.

It's not a flop. I'm just not done with it yet. I need to redo the _____.

Okay. But how long have you been waiting to work on it? Unless you've studied and learned a new way that you really want to try, it's unlikely you'll have more success just by repeating the same thing you did earlier. This isn't because you're lame. It might be because your original idea didn't match the project. Maybe you need a new idea for how to proceed at this part of the project. Or maybe you need to chalk it up to a great try at something that was harder than you'd thought it was going to be.

But I feel bad that I wasted all that money and time, and

so if I give up on the project I feel like I'm accepting the fact that I wasted money and time. And that is super depressing to think about.

What if it's true that you just used the money and time in a different way than you were planning to? What if it cost you $72 to experience not succeeding so that you could practice it—and what if the more you did it, the easier it got, and so your capacity grew, and you learned all kinds of interesting things about yourself—like how you stab yourself all the time when you hand sew because you can't find a thimble that actually fits your weirdly-shaped thumb; or how you actually never have asked anybody how to turn a corner when you're putting on the binding so maybe if you just read a couple of tiny pages about that it might go better next time; or how for some reason you believe that not wasting yarn is more important than protecting your own soul. This self-knowledge is easily worth $72.

All I have are projects that I'm part-way finished with. If I get rid of all of them, what will I do then?

Exactly.

We squirrel away our screw-ups like no other species. I'm pretty sure squirrels don't hoard rotten nuts. If you've got a full shelf in a closet that bulges with almost-nailed-its, let them go, ya'll. Throw away or give away or finish differently whatever is balled up in a shopping bag back there. Let the old projects die or wither if they want to. Don't force them to languish.

The best way I ever let go of failures is to turn them into something else. That usually involves ripping out what I've done—sort of rewinding—until I arrive at a place where I feel satisfied…and then starting again. But I've sent some right on over to the thrift store donation box, too. With the projects I had high hopes for, this "give away" process sometimes takes steps (like, literally, it requires me leaving it on the steps for a while—before I can get myself to put it in the pile that's heading to the donation center). It takes real emotional fortitude to declare that the thing you set out to make just isn't going to happen this time.

It takes guts. You can do it—think of the space in your soul that the message "that was supposed to look different" is taking up currently. Think of all that could fit in that space if the big fat, floppy reminder wasn't hanging around at your feet while you're trying to have some fun making things.

#6 Start Hoarding Ideas

Write down every idea—even a little one. It will be your friend down the road in some quiet window of time when your hands are ready but your head isn't. Treat your ideas like sweet directions for later. Keep an idea book so that you can sketch or make quick notes about the ideas that show up in unexpected moments. Be sure to grab good ideas as they come.

People who make things gather ideas. A little book for jotting notes or scrawling bad sketches is good for this. While walking from the car into your office you might flash on the picture of something your head just dreamed up for you. And, believe me, you won't remember it later. Grab your book, jot it down. Draw a quick, crummy sketch.

People who make things gather ideas. A little book for jotting notes or scrawling bad sketches is good for this. While walking from the car into your office you might flash on the picture of something your head just dreamed up for you. And, believe me, you won't remember it later. Grab your book, jot it down. Draw a quick, crummy sketch.

If you carry around an idea book, all that writing seeps into your regular day. There you are—in a car, probably. Or maybe in the dentist's office. And you've got your book. Some lady walks by with a tiny dog—the kind that's about as big as the hamster you had in fourth grade—and its little paws are scraping the snot out of her otherwise well-moisturized arm. And you think: *Dog Socks.*

And let me tell you that once the novocain hits and then wears off later, you won't remember that you had an idea to make dog socks. You'll see another little dog later, and you'll have a feeling like there's some itch you've got somewhere that you can't scratch. And if you drop everything, you might remember that you had an idea for the socks—but you likely won't see them as clearly as you did in that first flash. You won't remember that you had a thought for how to crochet them out of old shoe laces and that the clasp even came to you—you could see it in your mind.

Without that quick first sketch, you may sit down later to try to recapture that first thought, but you'll likely find yourself frustrated—sitting in a chair and staring, never coming up with quite the right thing, waiting for something to show itself that will be as inspired and ingenuitive as the idea that came when you were in the dentist's office.

This would all be handled if you just had a little book with you where you could scratch a picture of a dog sock or write the weird words DOG TOENAIL COVER THING. I'm just saying.

Go to the store. Buy a journal. Like right now—not in a week or eleven days, not when you have lots of money to buy something covered in llama suede: today—with about a buck and some change. Buy yourself an idea book.

An idea is worth a lot. And it's dodgy stuff to believe that you'll always get them at the exact moment when you can actually do something with them. Write them down.

#7 Sometimes Work Without a Pattern

T ry working without a pattern some time (even if the thought of giving up all of these beautifully tidy directions makes you sort of queasy.

Following a pattern can be really gratifying, but trust me here: sometimes walking right off the map is fun too. Just start building something some time. Build what your fingers feel like—with whatever they find.

You might be surprised by how much fun this is.

When you start keeping that book handy—the one

you're jotting your ideas in—then you'll notice that you maybe start making notes about the size-ish-ness of what you want to make, or the supplies you want to use. Or what sort of zippy pocket you'd like to go inside.

Try your hand at a sort of design-build process some time. You don't have to give up following instructions completely, just give this other thing a shot too. I've got nothing against a good set of instructions. But keep in mind that I'm only able to say this because I've never read an entire set of them.

Think of yourself as a kid with a box of tinker toys missing the instruction book. There is nothing to copy, just a pile of stuff to make with. If you like to sew, build with fabric. If you like to carve, then start at it. If you like to make paints out of strange tree roots, then get to mixing.

Because the beginning of a project can be the hardest part (in the sense that it's the easiest place to get completely stuck if you're nervous), then jumping in is really good practice. Practice beginning. Over and over again. Most things can be undone and re-done (or at least thrown out so you won't be reminded of them).

Practice chronicling what worked and what didn't as you went. You need to know. And tell the story of what you've done as you go. What do the ideas turn into? What worked? What tanked? Let yourself love the figuring out.

And too, if you're working with cheap goods and on projects that don't have to be spit out for somebody's birthday, then you won't cuss that much if it all goes sideways.

Do something easy. Make a napkin.

Try seeing something that you want in your head and then just tucking in and beginning. When I'm making a purse for myself, it doesn't matter how many inches wide the thing is. I don't have to know the number of inches. I can eyeball it for something close to what I think I'll want. I can hold it up next to another bag (the one that's just not as deep as I wish it were but is good for digging around in).

If the purse turns out wrong, nothing bad is going to happen to me. I will have learned about making purses. And the next one I make will be better than this one. And maybe I'll just use this one to store all my travel stuff in. Yeah. That's a good idea.

Remember: anything made with wood can be a door stop or a paper weight. Anything made with fabric can be a, um, napkin. Anything with glitter on it can be given to a two year old for a birthday gift. So these efforts aren't strictly headed for the waste bin.

Building is fun. You don't hear the voice of the person who's already figured it out ringing in your head the whole time, so your own ideas speak up and have a say.

What do you see in your head? And it's okay if you only see the backs of your eyelids. This doesn't mean you're lame. It likely means that you design in a different way than just copying whatever projects itself there. What do you keep staring at out in the world? What do you talk to other people about making? Make a little sketch of it. Draw how it could look, start to take some guesses at how it could come together. Give yourself the beginnings of a design of your own.

#8 See Time in Smaller Pieces

As busy people, the expectation that we would have the inspiration, the occasion, the energy, and the goods come to us all at once is just goofy. Lose it and plan otherwise.

Expect your creative life to be played out in small pieces. Not all of us will walk away from full-time jobs and step into six-hour stretches of open time. Let the small bits of time count.

There is a different way to think about what "counts" as creative time—and embracing it can bolster and encourage us. Sure, our time consists of precious moments of construction, but it can also include things that ready us for what we think of as "making time."

You've had all those other moments thinking of what you'd like to make, capturing it in a little book for later, a book that you haul with you wherever you are—back pocket, bottom of the purse, bike basket, backpack, whatever.

And all those thinking moments count.

You've had the moments where something caught your eye and you grabbed it (even without a clear plan). You let yourself add it to your stash of making goods. Those moments count.

Your brain is working as it passes by a stack of goods in your house—it's grabbing color combos and matching ideas it had three days ago to new stacks you just put there yesterday. Those thinking moments count.

Plus there's the time you spend telling your friends what you're making these days.

All those moments count as making time.

When you start adding those moments up, you might notice that you are living a life that has space for your creative self. And when you notice that you have made time for making in your life, you'll likely start making more of it.

Your making life spans more than just those two-hour-long sessions at the sewing machine or with the saw or in the backyard at your pottery wheel (the one you made out of an old lazy susan, a dull-edged blender and a broken chair).

Look at your days of the week. Where are the spots for quiet idea fishing? (You know—those times when you're having to wait around anyway.)Where are the spots for constructing? (Some chunk of time when it's no big deal to make a mess since everybody else is too.)

Look for small pieces. Don't try to find 3-hour blocks or whole-days-away or anything nutty like that. Look for in-between-times.

We can construct a making life out of small puzzle pieces of time if we want to. Sometimes we've got to really squint to find them, but little pieces of time are often there—even if they're just in 15 – 20 minutes spurts.

Find them. Claim them. Circle them and draw big arrows at them. Mark them as making time.

#9 Don't Settle for Expertise

Really the biggest challenge to our making lives is anything that looks like actual expertise or success. When we get so good at making something that everybody loves it and rushes up to us and wants to pay a gazillion dollars for it on the spot, that's when we need to get nervous about our making lives.

It's great to get really good at something, sure. But we need to pay close attention to our souls in these moments. As soon as we consistently begin to make things well—perfectly, we might even say—the part of us that expects perfection creeps back in. The stakes have skyrocketed when we weren't looking. And our small mistakes begin to look much bigger to us.

We are at risk of becoming stuck. This situation is particularly tricky, because we will look like the last people anyone would ever expect of being creatively stuck. But our hearts will feel the constraint of required success, and it's likely some part of us will start to drag its metaphoric feet, and everything about what we're good at making will start to become harder and harder for us to enjoy—not necessarily harder and harder for us to accomplish, but surely more difficult to find soul-quieting for us.

This is how and why people who get really good at one sort of art or craft need to stop everything regularly and go hunting to try something they don't know how to do. Sometimes we need to reset ourselves back to beginner just so that our creative selves can come up for some air, be allowed to try something in a low stakes way where everybody around isn't waiting with their own breath held to see the next amazing thing we're about to pull off.

Metal workers need to try weaving. Beaders need to do paper crafts. Watercolorists need to try embossing onto metal. We need to change up the goods and the techniques for ourselves regularly so we can keep remembering that perfection isn't the goal: making is.

Nobody even needs to know we're doing it. If our making lives have become public, it might be really important for us to have a private set of projects that we promise ourselves will never leave the house.

It's okay to sometimes do things that don't prove anything about our abilities—even when we have them.

Financial and social success are wonderful to accomplish in our making lives. They often relieve the tension of other pulls on our time. But they can backfire on us too. We need to stay beginners.

Don't settle into a single expertise on one kind of making—keep trying new things so that your soul has a chance to just play at what you're doing.

Go be a beginner. What's it gonna be? If you're good at one thing, what's the thing you don't know a thing about but have wanted to try? Go do something you're no good at.

#10 Find Your Show & Tell People

As you pursue your making life, you're going to need to find some people who are willing to listen to you talk about what you've discovered.

They might be people who are running after a maker's life too—but they might not be. They might have some other thing they love in their soul (like finding out the names of flowers they come across when they walk through parks). What they need to be is really interested in you, likely. They don't even need to be that interested in the particularities of what you're doing, although if you can find people who get the same buzz from vintage sheets you do, you're set.

Friends who are willing to tromp over into whatever corner you are making in and hear you say, "And then I made this. And then I made this. And then I made this."—these are people to keep close. Sometimes our hearts just really need to do an excited Show and Tell.

If you find people who will listen to you as you talk about these things, they will help you to continue becoming a person who values creative process. I hear lots of people talk about what they've made. I wish I heard more people talk about where they were stuck in the middle of making something. Because what am I supposed to say to a person who only tells me what they've successfully finished? "Um. Way to go." But to the person who talks to me about what they're scruffing their way through the middle of a project they're excited to pull off—well, we can talk for days. And it usually includes words like, "Me too! Me too!"

Practice talking about the process with people who understand and want to listen.

Whoever these friends are, treasure them. Consider them an important part of your life. You may not go to dinner with them much or even find that you invite them to your kids' birthday parties, but make sure you understand that their willingness to listen means that you are able to talk about what you're doing. And that talking—not just showing what you made as a final product—but the storytelling about the process you went through to make it: that is important stuff.

Some days you might wake up feeling a little crazy. *Does anybody else in the world want to turn old plastic straws and beach rocks into wind chimes?* And good friends who know you and get you will tell you things like "You bet."

There will be days when the people who understand how crucial your making life is to you will be the most important people you know. Some days you've got to take some deep breaths and decide that you're not crazy. Having good friends to do this with you helps.

For years I've been making things because I wanted to, and it's often felt a little piecemeal—like a significant part of my life, but without the steady money stream to prove to me that I really am supposed to do the stuff I love to do. It's taken an immeasurable amount of just deciding to keep at it and also self-talk.

And it's also taken the voices of some truly kind and loving people who have listened to me and nodded and sent me back in to keep at it. They've been cheerleaders, actually: unspastic, non-jumping, steadily encouraging cheerleaders willing to find the same joy in a quilt made out of old t-shirts that I do, even if they'd never have thought to make one themselves.

Who are your Show and Tell people? Draw a gorgeously detailed stick figure portrait of the lot of them if you need to: whatever it takes, know who they are and appreciate them. You need them.

NO
FAIRY DUST

NO FAIRY DUST

I used to tell my college writing students that I didn't have any fairy dust for them.

They would sort of glare at me when I would say this. "The only way to write is to write," I would say. Again: more glaring.

I tried to say this while smiling at them and sometimes patting them on the shoulder while I said it. I tried not to say it like I was annoyed at them for not knowing this. Because they'd heard something else for a really long time, and I knew it: that the only way to produce a perfect essay was to sit down and write one.

And it's what we've heard about most creative endeavors we've dreamed about pulling off: the only way to succeed is to make a perfect thing. And the only way to make a perfect thing, to do a perfect job, is to refuse to accept failure.

And this has worked for some of us. It had worked for my writing students in some ways. They had, after all, gotten into college. This had, they told me over and over again, been their goal. They wanted to get a good job, they said. And I would sit and smile and say things that made them twitch like, "The only way to write a really good essay is to start by writing a really BAD essay!" And they would look at each other. Some of them would shake their heads at me just so slightly that I'm sure they thought I couldn't see it.

Many of their stares became cold. And if one or two of them were brave enough to tell the truth out loud, we'd all end up in a really honest conversation about how hard it is to do something you don't feel good at—particularly when you had so many things you feel really good it.

And then I would tell them again that the only way to do it at all was to walk forward accepting the possibility that it might flop.

This did not match their efficient sensibilities.

"Why would I waste my time writing a bad essay? Can't you just tell me how to write a good one?"

"I am telling you, Grasshopper," I would say.

I was always taken aback by their anger. It wasn't their fear that bothered me. It was their anger. They seemed to have lived assured that they had the right to never fail. Or at least that they had a responsibility to never fail, and so my standing at the doorway marked, WOW, YOU MIGHT SCREW UP really bothered them. A few of them actively resented me for it.

Some of them stopped resenting me. These were the ones who heard me say, "I don't have any fairy dust" and understood that I meant this: The only way to get better at screwing up is to practice it.

The only way to get better at screwing up is to practice it.

They were the ones who were willing to give it a shot. They walked through the door of potential failure with me. It was really hard for them, but they gave it a shot. Maybe it would be just their scribbling on a scrap of paper for 10 minutes, but they'd put a foot in past the door jamb and feel that new sort of air on their shoes. And it counted. Even if it was just a little bit of trying something new, it mattered.

And I'm standing at that same doorway here. And I'm pointing to it for you. And I'm saying that if you believe that you have a responsibility to never fail, maybe you should consider claiming a different one. If your perfectionism is mostly what you're pulling off, well I'm suggesting that you consider having a different goal.

I know: I've got a lot of nerve. But I really think you can do it. I really think you can risk screwing up.

For some, this might seem an impossibility—like I'm suggesting that you move to France or stop being vegetarian or semi-non-Anglican. But it's maybe not as impossibly radical as it sounds.

I'm not suggesting that you quit your job. That you cut your hair. That you change your whole life.

I am suggesting that you risk something, a small thing at first—that you look out over the big green field of the years ahead of you and squint to see the space that could be yours if you'd claim it. What if you let maker be one of the important things that you are? Not the only thing that you are, just one of the important things. What if you invited it in?

What if you decided that it was okay to do with your hands what your heart's been saying for a long, long time that you ought to? And what if when you tried it the first or third or eleventh time and it didn't go so well, you knew that it was okay to tell yourself you were still allowed to do it a second and fourth and twelfth time anyway?

And what if it was okay that you never made any money at it? And what if it was okay if it took up some of the space in your house that could be used for something else? And what if you made something and it didn't look that great when you were finished, but it was really fun and relaxing while you were doing it? And what if sometimes you had work to do, but you put it aside for a bit and knew it would be there when you came back? And what if you decided that the fancy Talented People aren't the only ones who get to play? And what if you were nice to your family and you left for just little bits of time, and you weren't mad about it when you did? What if you just let yourself make a little something?

You wouldn't ever need any fairy dust if you just gave it a shot.

None of these suggestions are, well, fairy dust. They're all practice tips really—ideas for how to get started, offered with the honesty that you'll try one and won't like it at all. You'll try another, and it will seem like the best idea ever— and then you'll stop doing it. You'll need to be able to wake up a few days or weeks after you've fallen off the wagon and give it another go.

So just get started, friend. Just try some or all of these things. And then when they don't work, try them again. And then in a year, try them again.

Before you know it, you will be an absolute success at sailing through moments of what some would call "failure"—but we know differently, don't we?

So, when the one little edge of the polyester laptop cover that you made (in 12 minutes by stacking fabric at the speed of light, sewing three seams and then whipping it right side out)— turns out to be wonky and unfinished so that the inside fabric is poking out and the stitch is missed completely and it makes a little triangle of color in the bottom corner of the cover that somebody would call a mistake—when that happens, you stitch it down with hand sewing thread. You let it be there. And then, the final product only becomes sweeter in its particularity, in the memory of its once-ever making. Sweeter in the memory of sitting on the spray painted couch of your little sister's first condo and hearing the stories of her big, beautiful life. In that way there will never be another laptop cover like it for you. Its little surprise shout of color claims its own spot.

And maybe you stop looking at that laptop cover and wanting it to be any different than it is. You stop wanting it to look like the ones that you saw for sale at WhateverMart or like the ones you saw tagged on the thousands of pin boards you've been gathering for the last couple of years.

Maybe you'll look at it and think, "I made that." And you'll be glad about it. And you'll know for sure it's not the last thing you'll ever make.

And then someday when you're standing in line somewhere—at an airport maybe—somebody will say, "Cool laptop cover."

And you'll say, "Thanks, I made it."

And they'll say, "How do you have time for all that?"

And you'll have an answer.

EPILOGUE:
Pretend Interview with Barbara Walters

Barbara Walters: You know I don't do this much anymore, but I had to come down from the airplane that I fly around in faster than the speed of light to ensure that I don't age and ask you a few questions.

Ginger Hendrix: Sure, Barbara. Sure. Thanks for letting me sit with you here in your luxury jet on the tarmac.

B: As I read your book *TIME TO MAKE*, I was struck by the way that you seem to be challenging us to "grow a pair," as you say. Can you say more about that?

G: Did I end up including that phrase? I was sure I edited it out so that I would never have to hear someone like you say it out loud . . .you must have snagged an early draft.

I think I just mean, Barbara, that we're chicken sometimes, you know? We want to live one way, but then we find ourselves in this other life, and the other life is so FULL, full of things that we know are important, things we're usually doing for other people—things like making dinner and schlepping kids everywhere, but then when we sit in the dark on a Friday night where everybody's at somebody's basketball game and ask ourselves about our life, we are sort of tired. And sad.

B: Are those tears, Ginger?

G: No, not yet, Barbara—not yet. Right now I want to cry at the size of the ring you're wearing since I could probably put both of my sons through junior college with that thing.

B: Yes, it was a gift from Oprah. Christmas, I think. Insensitive, really. But beautiful. Back over to you, though, Ginger—how did you find yourself giving this clarion call to "live like a maker," as you say?

G: It really emerged from a lot of talking to myself. Not in the mentally ill way, of course.

B: Of course.

G: It was more that I found myself writing and writing about how important it is to live a life as full of creative expression as we can muster. And no matter how much of it I did—sewing, writing, singing and songwriting—I found myself still fighting back the urge to call it all a "hobby," to discount it somehow in my own life. I was asking, "Why can't my creative life be my life?" And it was, of course, the bank that kept answering that question.

B: "The bank," you say.

G: Yeah, I couldn't ever make enough cash at all the weird things I did to quit the full time job and just live my days doing the creative things that I loved to do.

B: But you're sitting here, aren't you? Did you finally get a lover's call from the bank?

G: Well, no. But I guess I finally stopped waiting by the phone.

B: Are you uncomfortable talking about your income, Ginger, and the way that you've never made any money doing your creative work and therefore think less of yourself than you wish you did?

G: Yes, Barbara. It's true. I am uncomfortable. I wish I could wake up every morning and just do the life I want to without second-guessing myself.

B: Maybe you should read your book, Ginger.

[*Long awkward silence where Barbara searches the face of Ginger to see if tears have appeared yet.*]

G: You know, Barbara, here's the thing: I have read my book. And the temptation is to believe that if I embrace a new way of thinking about my creative life, then I won't struggle any longer with these difficult questions of time and space and identity and cash—or with the way that our culture wants us to believe that our checkbooks and our business cards have the final say about who we are.

And even though I don't believe they get to tell me who I am, I notice that I still have to decide most days not to believe them. Because they haven't stopped talking to me.

I just don't think it's easy. And I'd hate for you—or anybody—to think that I'm trying to say it is.

B: It's so interesting, Ginger, because I would love to say that I hear defensiveness in your tone here, which I am listening for intently—but I don't. I hear the heart of a girl who woke up on a Saturday when she was young, laced up her tennis shoes and strode out of the backdoor to claim the green grass and embrace the possibilities of the world—

G: — Thank you, Barbara. I think—

B: —I see a woman who wants to embrace the inner space of the girl who believes in the possibilities but who has been worn down by the realities of a cold, dark world where money and power have the say and trample the green grass of even a hearty girl's hopes.

G: —I mean, I wouldn't say—

B: I look at you and I see myself, Ginger. I see a young woman who wants to stop the world in its tracks, sit it down in a room of some production team's making, ask it difficult questions, maybe help it find a tear or two it didn't know it was holding back. We just want to help people see themselves, don't we?

G: Yeah, I guess you're right…are those tears I see, Barbara?

B: Yes, Ginger, they are.

[*Man in tux brings in a box of tissue. Ginger receives this as it's intended: a signal to go. She quickly gets up, makes up an excuse for why she has to leave so abruptly, "I gotta go pick up my kids from shleznikelfufgen...," she says. Barbara sputters a semi-gracious acceptance of the shift in her plans, dabbing her eyes quickly and nodding her head, saying something about sending the book to Oprah to read. And Ginger walks out to the opening of the hatch, sees the stairs and the glittery carpet that's been laid there for her, sees the flatness of Nevada stretching out like a possibility, the waves of heat rising up off the asphalt and walks down the stairs and out into the hard, hot day. Ready.*]

INDEXES
AND
LISTS

ACTIVITY INDEX

Things to do so that you start listening to a more real part of yourself and not that busy, distracted, carb-eating part of yourself that's always driving your decisions...

(WRITE) & (DRAW)

(go do this)

THINGS THAT COUNT AS MAKING

Gluing anything to anything.
Hammering stuff.
Things you make with
   wood or plastic trash.
Singing.
Expressive polka.
Sand candles.
Sand castles.
Gardening.
Cooking.
Keeping bees.
All kinds of stitchery.
Sewing by hand.
Sewing with a machine.
Quilt making.
Quilt fixing.
Macramé.
Wood burning.
Wood carving.
Embroidering socks.
Lengthening pants in a
   lighthearted way.
Playing the cello.
Crocheting rugs.
Weaving.
Interpretive dance.
Paper crafts.
Anything with scissors
   that's fun.

Making jelly.
Marker art.
Watercolor.
Oil paints.
Calligraphy.
Making stuff out of old ties.
Daisy chains.
Beer alchemy.

Now you add some:

_____

_____

_____

_____

_____

_____

_____

AN INDEX OF TRUSTWORTHY VOICES

You can google your heart out to find directions to make just about anything now. Lots of us have posted free tutorials and many of those will walk you right through the process of making something.

One of the things that's harder to find online are consistent voices that offer help but also don't flaunt perfection. That doesn't mean they're not making good-looking stuff. It just means that when we go to their sites, we don't immediately curl up into a ball from an attack of Oh My Good Lord Why Doesn't My Bathroom Look That Pretty.

They're trustworthy voices. They seem to be as interested in the way they talk about making as they are about what they're making. This list is sort of short, but it's meant to get you rolling making your own. Pay attention to who you're watching. If they don't love wonk, reconsider how much eyeball time to give them. Require it for yourself—don't let images of somebody else's perfect-looking projects stand in the way of your making life.

You can start with these trustworthy voices if you'd like …

Diane Gilleland
CRAFTYPOD
craftypod.com

Sister Diane is a solid voice for the honest process of making. She offers final product tutorials and lots of good advice—but most of all she is a consistently encouraging online presence for people who are setting out to make things.

Jenny Lawson
THE BLOGGESS
thebloggess.com

She's a craft blogger? Nope. But she writes consistently and honestly about real things. And also she is always making things—just look closely: They're often weird posters and touched-up pictures of her cat fighting a stuffed, clothed rat.

Kristin Link & Beth Wilson
SEW MAMA SEW
sewmamasew.com

Beth and Kristin have built a fantastic community for people who love thread. They offer lots of ideas in a range of styles from a huge line-up of makers. Best of all, they seem most interested in pulling people together to tackle creative projects.

Thank you.

I've learned from many years as a Young Life Volunteer, my membership in the co-op, my spot in the book club, my place on the ETT, from teaching with the Sustain community, my years proofing the OG newsletter, and from being married to Pete that all real efforts are collaborations...even the ones that don't look like it; they're teamwork. That was surely true of this book project.

So thanks for the full-blown-cheering-on-ing to Bonnie and Jamie, my Project Doulas (stationed in Eden and Los Olivos). And thanks to Auntie Ann who always knew I would get to do this some day. And to Ash for being a pal who makes me braver at everything.

And to the huge choir of friends who read early drafts and listened to me talk and generally said "You're not crazy" to me for a couple of years as the thing came together. And big thanks to my Bloggish People Friends (BPF's) at Wienerdog Tricks who read the earliest of my thoughts on these questions and kept wanting me to say more. Really: thanks, you guys.

The highest of high fives to Ashley Self, Best Editor Ever. (Never. Fired.) Big thanks to Krystina Montemurro for the early layout and to Rocki deLlamas for book cover goodness and all around Amazing Creative Telepathy. And to Ashley Blake for taking the first decent picture of me since my 2nd grade school photo.

And to All These Kids: *May All Your Future Sandwiches Be Made By You Without A Speck of Resentment that I Taught You to Care For Yourself While I Was Typing.* I really like you all.

And thanks to Pete for his kind willingness to back me. All the time. For all these years.

GINGER HENDRIX once made a couch cover out of old polyester, once wrote and recorded a CD for kids, once learned to cook by hacking at low-fat magazine recipes (and then just doubling the cheese), once sewed at least 30 aprons out of strange scraps, salvaged old quilts into new ones, and even tried making a lamp out of an old coffee pot. She has been known to teach writing and sewing. She writes the blog Wienerdog Tricks at gingerhendrix.com.

34367776R00119

Made in the USA
Middletown, DE
20 August 2016